The Apologia
of
Robert Keayne

The Apologia of Robert Keayne

THE LAST WILL AND TESTAMENT
OF ME, ROBERT KEAYNE, ALL OF IT WRITTEN
WITH MY OWN HANDS AND BEGAN BY
ME, MO: 6: 1: 1653, COMMONLY
CALLED AUGUST

The Self-Portrait of a Puritan Merchant

Edited by

Bernard Bailyn

GLOUCESTER, MASS.

PETER SMITH

1970

THE APOLOGIA OF ROBERT KEAYNE
Copyright © 1964, The Colonial Society of Massachusetts
Printed in the United States of America.
This book was originally published as a chapter in *Publications of
The Colonial Society of Massachusetts*, Volume XLII, *Transactions
1952–1956*, published in 1964 by The Colonial Society of Massachu-
setts. It is here reprinted by arrangement.
First HARPER TORCHBOOK edition published 1965 by
Harper & Row, Publishers, Incorporated
49 East 33rd Street, New York, New York 10016

Reprinted, 1970, by Permission of
Bernard Bailyn

CONTENTS

INTRODUCTION
by
Bernard Bailyn

ON 1 August 1653, Robert Keayne of Boston, a retired merchant of great piety, began to write the final version of his Last Will and Testament.[1] It was not an easy task. The bequests he had in mind for the members of his immediate family (his wife, son, and granddaughter) were complicated. Other relatives also had to be properly provided for, servants had to be rewarded, friends acknowledged. Moreover, the merchant had long ago decided that one-third or thereabouts of all his property would be given as a gift for specific uses to the town and the commonwealth. The most elaborate precautions must be taken to see that this pious intent would not be thwarted.

These were difficulties enough. But they were simple next to the task of explanation and justification that faced the merchant. No one, either in Old England or New, could have denied that God had blessed Keayne's worldly endeavors. Starting life as a butcher's boy in Windsor, near London, receiving "no portion from my parents or friends to begin the world withal," Keayne had triumphed over countless adversities, surviving financial losses "sufficient to have broken the back of any one man in the country," and now stood firm in his declining years, a man of substance, worth perhaps £4,000.[2] And yet, for all of this, his life had been cursed, mainly, it seemed, by this very success. For years he had been hounded by jealous hypocrites who had attacked his right to his own hard-earned wealth. They claimed that he had gotten his fortune by "corrupt practices": by usury, by taking advantage of buyers' needs, by putting his own gain ahead of the common good. This cry had been heard even in England and had risen in intensity in the first years of the merchant's career in the Bible Commonwealth. The climax had come within four years of his emigration, in 1639, when public opinion had suddenly mobilized against him and struck a terrible, unforgettable blow. The events of that year "carried on with so much bitterness and indignation . . . contrary or beyond the quality and desert of the complaints that came against me" had never ceased to haunt him.

[1] For an annotated biographical sketch of the merchant and an extensive analysis of his Will, see *William and Mary Quarterly*, third series, VII (1950), 568–587.
[2] Unless otherwise noted, all quotations are from the text of the Will that follows.

It had been hard enough to have been charged in the General Court with "taking six-pence in the shilling profit; in some above eight-pence; and in some small things above two for one." It had been worse still to be fined £200 for this supposed misdemeanor, even if later the sum had been reduced to £80. But far worse had been the insistence of his accusers that he was guilty not only of a crime but also of a sin. They had brought the case to the elders of the First Church in Boston, who had conducted an "exquisite search" to determine "how far I was guilty of all those clamors and rumors that then I lay under." And to his everlasting chagrin they had admonished him severely "in the name of the Church for selling his wares at excessive rates, to the dishonor of God's name, the offense of the General Court, and the public scandal of the country." Only by a humiliating "penetential acknowledgment" a few months later was he able to reconcile himself officially with the Church.[3]

For fourteen years the recollection of this disgrace had pursued him, and now as he prepared to draw up his Last Will and Testament it lurked at the edges of his thoughts. Not that the usury trial had been his only misfortune. Three years later he had again been haled through the courts by those who believed Mrs. Sherman when she insisted that Keayne had stolen her sow. The case against him had been weak, but his unpopularity was great. Deputies and magistrates disagreed when the case was taken on appeal to the General Court, and so intense was the controversy that the two groups of legislators could proceed only separately, and hence Keayne's woes were at the origin of Massachusetts' bicameralism. His son Benjamin's marriage to the "unnatural and unhappy," "proud and disobedient" Sarah Dudley had ended in separation. And in 1652 the merchant himself, recently elevated to a Suffolk County judgeship, had come into absolute disgrace. The General Court convicted him of having "been three times drunk, and to have drunk to excess two times." His resignation from the bench was promptly accepted, the legislators "judging him not meet to continue therein."[4]

Yet when he came to draw up his final testament these miseries were not foremost in his mind. The engrossing, gripping episode of his life was still the trial of 1639 and his mind kept slipping back to it as he prepared to dispose of his property.

Burdened with caring for his family's welfare, repaying his debt to

[3] Records of the First Church of Boston (copy in Massachusetts Historical Society), 12, 14.
[4] N. B. Shurtleff, ed., Records of the Governor and Company of the Massachusetts Bay in New England (Boston, 1853–1854), III. 278.

society, and filing with posterity a final plea in the usury proceedings, Keayne proceeded to write out his Last Will. It became an exhaustive apologia. As he wrote unforseen contingencies came to mind. He felt a compulsive need to follow each shilling through the course of transfer, anticipating all possible misuses. His thoughts rushed on faster than his pen, spilling through the obstructions of syntax and punctuation, pouring out in grammarless floods of provisions, qualifications, claims, arguments, rebuttals, charges, and pleas. The hours of his labors became days and weeks. For five months he labored and when he finally signed and sealed the last page he had written a treatise of 50,000 words which later filled no less than 158 pages of the Suffolk County probate records.

Keayne's Last Will and Testament is an extraordinary document. Hidden in its helter-skelter, half-incoherent prose lies not only a moving human story but also rare historical evidences, the more valuable because written by an unselfconscious chronicler. They reveal as few records do intimate views of the early seventeenth century: a common man's understanding of leading points in Calvinist theology; Puritan philanthropy, the "stewardship of wealth" in operation; the bookkeeping system of a merchant-tradesman; social conditions in Massachusetts during the lifetime of the first generation. Above all, Keayne's Will illustrates vividly the actual influence of Calvinist thought in its New England Puritan form upon the life of trade.

Driven by the need to justify his life, Keayne sketched a self-portrait of the Puritan merchant. It is a rounded picture, complex with the shadings of reality. Here are the economic virtues embedded in the Protestant ethic—virtues, we have been told, intimately involved with the "spirit of capitalism." But they are wound in among counter-forces that checked and controlled their free play in behalf of social ideals more medieval than modern: the conviction that the success of trade was to be measured as much by its contribution to the community's as to the merchant's welfare, and that the leaders of both church and state were charged by God with the supervision of economic as well as religious and political activity.

Thus Keayne displays an interest in records and accounts—witnesses of "economic rationalism"—so intense as to appear at times pathological. He devotes pages of the Will to a description of his bookkeeping system. The overseers must be told about an inventory book, a receipt book, a day book, a pocket book, two number books, three debt books, a farm book, a rent book, two cash containers, and numerous files and boxes of bills and papers. His whole life, he declares at one point, has been recorded in one or another of his accounts. And he makes explicit the relation between this business rationalism and his spiritual career:

Happy yea more happy would it have been for me if I had been as careful and as exact in keeping an account of my sins and the debts I owe to God and of that spiritual estate between God and my own soul [as he has been in keeping his business accounts] that I could as easily have made it appear to others or to myself when I gained or when I lost and to have taken as much pains this way as in the other, which, though I cannot truly say I have altogether neglected or omitted, yet comparatively I may justly say I have been greatly deficient in that one thing necessary.

Rarely do we find such a devotion to one's "calling" or such a conviction, however hedged about, that worldly success is an outward sign of spiritual grace. It is with confidence that he rests his case with God, for

I have many testimonies in my spirit that He hath righted me therein, not only in the hearts and judgments of many men that knew and heard of those [usury] proceedings, but also in my very outward estate, that though some intended it for my great hurt, yet God hath been pleased to turn it to my good so that I have not since fared the worse nor lost by it but hath since carried me through many and great engagements with comfort.

And the proper conduct of life? Keayne is most specific. His voluminous accounts, he boasts, will

testify to the world on my behalf that I have not lived an idle, lazy, or dronish life, nor spent my time wantonly, fruitlessly, or in company-keeping as some have been too ready to asperse me, or that I have had in my whole time either in Old England or New many spare hours to spend unprofitably away or to refresh myself with recreations, except reading and writing hath been a recreation to me, which sometimes is mixed with pain and labor enough. Rather I have studied and endeavored to redeem my time as a thing most dear and precious to me and have often denied myself in such refreshings that otherwise I might lawfully have made use of.

But at the same time Keayne venerates the authority of the magistrates and church elders and shares with them the terms in which worldly success must be justified. He assumes the validity of the concept of usury and the jurisdiction of the General Court and the First Church over such matters; he argues merely that the charges against him were falsified by a vindictive individual. His aim throughout is to prove his piety, the purity of his intentions, and his scrupulous regard for the community's welfare. His description of his shocked reactions to the usury trial rings with sincerity:

... the newness and strangeness of the thing, to be brought forth into an open court as a public malefactor, was both a shame and an amazement to me. It was the grief of my soul (and I desire it may ever so be in a greater measure) that any act of mine (though not justly but by misconstruction) should be an occasion of scandal to the Gospel and profession of the Lord Jesus, or that myself should be looked at as one that had brought any just dishonor to God (which I have endeavored long and according to my weak ability desired to prevent), though God hath been pleased for causes best known to Himself to deny me such a blessing. And if it had been in my power I should rather have chosen to have perished in my cradle than to have lived to such a time.

What was the effect of Puritanism on the business lives of merchants like Robert Keayne? It was not a simple, singular influence. It encouraged while it discouraged; it justified while it condemned. It rationalized, perhaps, the urge to accumulate worldly goods, but at the same time it confined this impulse to limits set and enforced by both church and state. Calvinism in its New England Puritan form accounts not for a new "spirit of capitalism" but rather for a delicate balance of tensions in the life of the pious merchant—a balance as heavily weighted with medieval business ethics as with Protestant worldly asceticism. The growth of capitalistic society involved not the perpetuation but the destruction of this Puritan balance.

Keayne's strategy in forcing a final hearing of his case at the bar of posterity was shrewdly chosen: "a will will be read and made known and may be perused, searched, or copied out by any when other writings will be more hid and obscured." His Last Will was carefully examined by his overseers and legatees; it was studied by the committee appointed to carry out his bequest to the town of Boston; it featured in the legal tribulations of his granddaughter; and it was excerpted into the records of Harvard College. Two centuries later a rising interest in American antiquities led to the publication of the entire Will in all its grammatical and orthographical confusion by the Boston Record Commissioners in their tenth *Report* (Boston, 1886). Since then use has occasionally been made of the document by antiquarians and specialists in seventeenth-century or business history.

Yet the Will has not reached the general audience it deserves. In part this is due to the character of the single printed version. The tenth *Report* is not readily accessible and the Will there reproduced can be read only with the greatest difficulty. The type is minuscule and the text is entirely lacking in punctuation, clotted with ampersands, superior letters, and archaic spellings, and tangled with parentheses and qualifying clauses.

The purpose of the present publication[5] is to make this strange and valuable document available in a readable version. For that reason I have taken liberties with the text, attempting to impose order on the confusion of the Will without sacrificing Keayne's thought. The revisions have been, first, to change all spellings to their modern forms; second, to introduce punctuation and paragraphing throughout; third, to divide the text into convenient sections; and fourth, to clear out the verbal underbrush by occasional cuttings and insertions. Except for articles and the single words that relate directly to punctuation (conjunctions and relative pronouns) all additions and deletions have been indicated. Brackets enclose substitutions as well as additions.

[5] Based on a comparison of the text in the tenth *Report* and the handwritten copy in the first volume of the Suffolk County Probate Records (1892).

The Apologia
of
Robert Keayne

THE LAST WILL AND TESTAMENT
OF ME, ROBERT KEAYNE, ALL OF IT WRITTEN
WITH MY OWN HANDS AND BEGAN BY
ME, MO: 6: 1: 1653, COMMONLY
CALLED AUGUST

I, Robert Keayne, citizen and merchant tailor of London by freedom
and by the good providence of God now dwelling at Boston in New England in America, being at this time through the great goodness of my
God both in health of body and of able and sufficient memory, yet considering that all flesh is as grass that must wither and will return to the
dust and that my life may be taken away in a moment, therefore that I
may be in the better readiness—freed from the distracting cares of the
disposing of my outward estate . . . [at] the time of sickness or day of
death when the mind should be taken up with more serious and weighty
considerations—I do therefore now in my health make, ordain, and declare this to be my last will and testament and to stand and to be as effec-
tual as if I had made it in my sickness or in the day or hour of my death,
which is in manner and form following.

[Thanks to a Merciful God: His Declaration of Faith]

First and before all things, I commend and commit my precious soul
into the hands of Almighty God, who not only as a loving creator hath
given it unto me when He might have made me a brute beast, but also as
a most loving father and merciful saviour hath redeemed it with the precious blood of His own dear son and my sweet Jesus from that gulf of
misery and ruin that I by original sin and actual transgressions had
plunged it into. Therefore, I renounce all manner of known errors, all
Popish and prelatical superstitions, all anabaptistical enthusiasms and
familistical delusions, with all other feigned devices and all old and new
upstart opinions, unsound and blasphemous errors, and other high imagi-
nations that exalt themselves against the honor and truth of God in the
way of His worship and ordinances and against the dignity and scepter
of the Lord Jesus Christ my Saviour.

I do further desire from my heart to renounce all confidence or expectation of merit or desert in any of the best duties or services that ever
I have, shall, or can be able to perform, acknowledging that all my righteousness, sanctification, and close walking with God, if it were or had
been a thousand times more exact than ever yet I attained to, is all pol-
luted and corrupt and falls short of commending me to God in point of

my justification or helping forward my redemption or salvation. They deserve nothing at God's hand but hell and condemnation if He should enter into judgment with me for them. And though I believe that all my ways of holiness are of no use to me in point of justification, yet I believe they may not be neglected by me without great sin, but are ordained of God for me to walk in them carefully, in love to Him, in obedience to His commandments, as well as for many other good ends. They are good fruits and evidences of justification. Therefore, renouncing though not the acts yet all confidence in those acts of holiness and works of sanctification performed by me, I look for my acceptance with God and the salvation of my soul only from the merits or righteousness of the Lord Jesus Christ, and from the free, bountiful, and undeserved grace and love of God in Him. And though this faith in me in respect of application for my own comfort is very weak and feeble, yet I look up to my God in Jesus Christ to strengthen it. And though the sinful failings and weaknesses of my own life have been great and many, and [though] neither myself nor family in respect of close walking with Him hath been so with God as it ought to be (for which I have and shall still desire and endeavor to judge and condemn myself in His sight, and not to allow myself in any ways of evil knowingly), yet I look up to His throne of grace and mercy in the blood of Jesus Christ with some hope and confidence that He will both pardon and subdue them. In this faith alone I desire both to live and die and to continue therein to my life's end.

This faith in the Lord Jesus Christ hath been most plainly and sweetly taught in these churches of New England, in which place, though I met with many and deep sorrows and variety of exercises of spirit and hard measures offered to me, yet with unrepentant thoughts I desire to acknowledge it for a great blessing and undeserved favor of God that He hath brought me hither to enjoy His presence in the beauties of holiness, and to see His walkings in His holy sanctuary. And though there may be failings both in our civil government and churches (for all men have their weaknesses and the best societies of men have their imperfections, so that still there will be some things to be amended and reformed as God shall be pleased to discover new light and means to do it), yet I do unfeignedly approve of the way of the churches of Jesus Christ and the civil government that God hath here set up amongst us, and rejoice therein, as a way that both I pray for and doubt not but God will bless. According to that light that I have received or that which I ever read or heard of, it is one of the best and happiest governments that is this day in the world.

This being premised in respect of my soul and my faith in Jesus Christ,

I do next commit my body to the earth (and to comely and decent burial), there to rest till my loving Saviour by His almighty power shall raise it up again, at which time I confidently believe it shall be reunited to my own soul. There it shall receive according to the works that I have done in this life according as they have been good or evil in the sight of God or according to that faith and confidence that I have in the free grace and merits of the Lord Jesus Christ.

As for my burial, I shall not desire any great outward solemnity to be used further than that which shall be decent and civil as becomes Christians, knowing that extraordinary solemnities can nothing add to the peace or benefit of the deceased. Yet, having been trained up in military discipline from my younger years and having endeavored to promote it the best I could since God hath brought me into this country, and seeing He hath been pleased to use me as a poor instrument to lay the foundation of that noble society of the Artillery Company in this place which hath so far prospered by the blessing of God as to help many with good experience in the use of their arms and more exact knowledge in the military art, and hath been a nursery to raise up many able and well experienced soldiers that hath done since good service for their country; therefore, to declare my affections to that exercise and the society of soldiers, I shall desire to be buried as a soldier in a military way, if the time and place of my death and other occasions may suit thereunto.[6] This I leave to the discretion of my executors and friends.

[*Main Gifts to His Family*][7]

As for the goods of this life which the Lord of His abundant mercy, His rich and undeserved favor, hath bestowed and reserved to me the greatest of sinners and the unworthiest of all His servants, I dispose of them in manner following.

Imprimis, my will is that all such debts as I do or shall justly owe to any person or persons at the time of my death shall be truly and carefully paid by my executors within as short time after my decease as convenient-

[6] Keayne had become a member of the Honourable Artillery Company of London in 1623, and had been a founder and the first captain of the Ancient and Honorable Artillery Company of Massachusetts. G. Goold Walker, *The Honourable Artillery Company* [*of London*] (London, 1926), 42–43; Oliver A. Roberts, *History of the ... Ancient and Honorable Artillery Company of Massachusetts* (Boston, 1895–1901), I. 1–21.

[7] The complicated history of the Keayne family estate up to the death of the merchant's granddaughter in 1704 has been sketched by Edmund S. Morgan in "A Boston Heiress and Her Husbands: A True Story," these *Publications*, XXXIV. 499–513.

ly may be. Which debts of mine at this time doth amount to about one hundred and fifty pounds besides what I owe unto the poor box. The particulars of this and the persons to whom I am indebted my executors and overseers may find in a long paper book in my closet at Boston with a white parchment cover, entitled my inventory book, in which the particulars of my whole estate from year to year with all that I owe and all debts that are owing to me is briefly set down under my own hand. This will be a direction to them in all my affairs. These debts of mine, if God be pleased to spare me health [during] the next spring, I hope I shall pay the most of them myself except that only which I owe to the poor box, being about eighty pounds.

For the better effecting and accomplishing of this my last will and testament my will and desire is that presently after my death or burial . . . there may be a true inventory taken of all my lands, houses, cattle, movable goods, books, household stuff of all sorts, of all my wares, merchandise, ready money, plate, rings, jewels, beaver, wearing apparel, tools or any such like, of all the corn I have at home or at my farm, with all things there, of all the debts that are owing to me, especially those that I account good. (And which they be you may see not only in my several debt books but [in] the abridgment of them all—except housing, household stuff and movables, plate, tools, etc.—in that inventory book before mentioned.) [My desire is] that all these things may be equally valued and priced by such indifferent and just men that have good skill and experience in the several kinds of goods that are to be valued, and if more convenient that an oath may be given to them to value and price them according to the common worth and value that such goods and lands shall bear at that time in this country as near as their best judgment and skill therein shall lead them to. . . . As my executors may have no wrong so neither would I have my legacies and gifts swallowed up [by] an apprehension or report that I have given away more than my estate will bear, and that I have made a great show of charity and have nothing or not enough to perform it with.

This inventory of my estate being so taken and all things valued equally and without partiality and not at half what they are duly worth, as is the use of many, [my desire then is that] so much be deducted out of the sum total as my funeral charges and my debts that I shall owe at that time may come to, which my book entitled creditor and debitor in my closet at Boston and other debt books and books of account will clearly discover, especially that inventory book first mentioned. Which sum being set by in the account for discharge of my debts, the residue and remainder of my estate I dispose of as followeth.

Imprimis, the third of all my lands and housing both at Boston and at my farm at Rumney Marsh[8] or anywhere else that I shall be possessed of at the time of my death I give and bequeath unto my dear and loving wife Mrs. Anne Keayne,[9] to hold and enjoy with all the profits of them or that shall arise from them during her natural life, according to the last law of our General Court made concerning widows' doweries. This I believe will be a large and comfortable maintenance for her, a great if not the greatest part of my estate lying in my housing and lands and there being no engagements or encumbrances yet upon any part of my lands. [Otherwise,] I would make such an addition to it as might make her life in respect of outward things both peaceable and comfortable. Nor shall I forget some other pledges of my love to her.

This third for my wife being premised and my funeral charges and debts being provided for as I have before mentioned, the rest of my whole estate both personal and real, with my lands, housing, and all the other things belonging to my estate, I divide into two parts, the one part whereof I give and bequeath unto my well beloved and only son Benjamin Keayne; the other part of my estate (I mean the just or due value of it) I reserve as my own right to dispose of as I please, which is as herein shall after be expressed.

... I am not ignorant that formerly there hath been many clamors and evil reports raised up against me here and elsewhere as if I had got my estate by unjust dealing and wronging of others. That all might take notice that I durst not allow myself in any such known wickedness as hath been falsely reported against me, I did in some of my former wills and also in my last before this, of anno 1649, ... set apart two hundred pounds out of my own estate, that if any man or woman (not knowing but that I might have died long before this time) young or old, in Old England or New, could justly challenge or make it appear by good proof or reason that I had in anything unjustly wronged or defrauded them,

---

[8] For a description of this particular property and an account of its subsequent history, see Mellen Chamberlain, *Documentary History of Chelsea* (Boston, 1908), chaps. xix-xxi.

[9] The proper spelling of seventeenth-century names is often a puzzle as there was little consistency in usage. Hannah, Anna, and Anne were used almost interchangeably. Since Keayne himself was more or less consistent in calling his wife Anne and his granddaughter Hannah (though the latter herself apparently preferred Anna) I shall follow his preference.

that they might have had full satisfaction allowed them, though I know of no such things that can justly be laid to my charge, nor any pretense of show of it [which], if I were alive to answer for myself, I should [not] easily clear and remove. But having now lived in New England this 17 or 18 years where there is an open passage in church and commonwealth where any that are unjustly wronged may easily right themselves if I should obstinately refuse to do them right, and none such having appeared in so many years, I think it needless to continue any longer what I formerly sequestered out of my estate for such ends. If any should come with such pretenses after I am dead, the falseness of them may the more justly be suspected in that they came not while I was alive. I speak of debts and unjust frauds, not of human infirmities and failings which may be common to myself as to other men.

[Gifts to the Public: A Conduit and a Town House Comprising a Market Place, Court Room, Gallery, Library, Granary, and an Armory]

I have long thought and considered of the want of [two] necessary things of public concernment which may not be only commodious but very profitable and useful for the town of Boston: a market place and a conduit.[1] The one [would be] a good help in danger of fire, the want of which we have found by sad and costly experience not only in other parts of the town where possibly they have better supply for water but in the heart of the town about the market place. The other [would be] useful for the country people that come with their provisions for the supply of the town, that they may have a place to sit dry in and warm both in cold, rain, and dirty weather, and may have a place to leave their corn or any other things that they cannot sell safe till they come again. This would be both an encouragement to the country to come in and a great means to increase trading in the town. [I have also thought] to have [in the same building] some convenient room or two for the courts to meet in, both in winter and summer, and also for the townsmen and commissioners of the town. In the same building or the like there may also be a convenient room for a library and a gallery or some other handsome room for the elders to meet in and confer together when they have occasion to come to the town for any such end, as I perceive they have many. Then

---

[1] The provisions that follow led to the construction of Boston's first town house; the conduit project was less successful. See Josiah H. Benton, *The Story of the Old Boston Town House 1658-1711* (Boston, 1908).

in the same building there may be also a room for an armory to keep the arms of the Artillery Company and for the soldiers to meet in when they have occasion.

Now it [may] not be thought convenient by the elders and deacons or guides of the town that all these conveniences should be under one roof or in one place of the town and that there be some places already built that may conveniently be used or fitted up with small cost for some of these purposes, as in the meeting house for a granary or armory and other places in it for the magistrates and commissioners to meet in as they do sometimes. It is true in the summer they may, [but] in the winter they cannot for want of chimneys and fires. It would be necessary and more convenient (and the town hath been often speaking about it, to have such a building for such uses, though yet it hath not been accomplished) if there were a place fitted on purpose and set apart for such public uses. And if advice were taken with some skillful and ingenious workmen and some others that have good heads in contriving of buildings, such as Mr. Broughton, Mr. Clarke the surgeon, etc., there might such a model be drawn up that one fabric or building may be easily contrived that would conveniently accommodate all these uses without extraordinary cost and yet may be so done as would be a great ornament to the town as well as useful and profitable otherwise.

But if the chief of the town should be of another mind then I should propose this, that the conduit and market house be set in the market place somewhere between Mr. Cogan's house and mine or anywhere in that great street between Mr. Parker's house and Mr. Brenton's, or rather Mr. Webb's, if it should be judged there to be more convenient. These two may handsomely be contrived in one building in which possibly may be some other convenient rooms fit for some of the uses before mentioned besides. And for those which that place cannot supply, as for a library and for a gallery or long-room for the divines and scholars to meet and confer together upon any occasion, it may be contrived to be set all along on the foreside of the meeting house joining to it on the one side, and the other side to be supported with pillars so the rooms about may be for court meetings at the one side and the elders at the other. The open room between the pillars, being either paled or boarded on the ground, may serve for merchants, masters of ships, and strangers as well as the town to meet in at all times to confer about their business and occasions.

This I conceive would be very advantageous to the town and may be so contrived and set forth that it will be no disgrace or encumbrance to the meeting house but a great ornament to it. But if it should be thought not convenient to have it in the front of the meeting house, it may accomplish the same ends if placed on that side of the meeting house from Sergeant Williams' shop to Deacon Truesdale's house. Or, if a building placed in one of these two places may accomplish all the ends before mentioned save only the conduit, then a large conduit may be set up alone about the place where the pillary stands and the other about the meeting house as [described] before. Which [of these,] I leave to the best contrivement of the town and the elders and deacons. If the town shall think meet to go about it and improve this building or buildings for the several uses before mentioned, only the granary may be in any other place of the town as shall be thought convenient. I stand not upon that, though my own judgment leads me to think that some places or place about the common market or near to it will be most suitable for many reasons. I say, towards the building of these convenient places.

Item. I give and bequeath three hundred pounds in good merchantable pay the one third part thereof when the frame is brought to the place and raised, or some part of [this sum] before ... the frame is in some forwardness, if need be; the second part when the chimneys are built, the house covered and closed in round, and all the floors laid; and the last third part when it is quite finished, provided that it be gone about and finished within two or three years at the most after my decease. And if any of these, either a conduit or market house, should be set up before my death by the town or any other in the place or places above mentioned, then my gift shall remain good either for some addition to the same work or for the accomplishing of those other works by me mentioned that are not done by others, with a rebating proportionable to what is or shall be before done by the town or any other person.

Now that these things may not be only for a show or a name and when finished prove as shadows and stand as empty rooms without substance, that they may be improved for the uses that I aim at and intend though my estate is not such as whereby I am able to do for such public benefit what I desire and would be willing to do if I had it, yet for example's sake and encouragement of others (especially of our own town which will have the benefit of it and such in the town that have public spirits and some comfortable estates to help on such works) I shall be willing to cast in my mite and bring my lime and hare [so that] possibly God may stir up the hearts of others to bring in their badger skins and silk and others more costly things that the work may go on and prosper in so small a beginning—therefore, to the granary I give and bequeath one hundred pounds to be paid in corn and that to be improved for a public stock to such uses and ends as I shall hereafter mention. Next, the library and gallery for divines and scholars to meet in being finished, I give and bequeath to the beginning of that library my 3 great writing books which are intended as an exposition or interpretation of the whole Bible; also a 4th great writing book in which is an exposition on the prophecy of Daniel, of the Revelations, and the prophecy of Hosea, not long since began. All these books are written with my own hand so far as they be writ. And I could desire that some able scholar or two that is active and diligent and addicted to reading and writing were ordered to carry on the same work by degrees as they have leisure and opportunity, in the same method and way as I have begun (if a better be not advised to), [especially] if it shall be esteemed for the profit of it to young students (though not so to more able and learned divines in these knowing times), worth the labor as I have and do find it to myself worth all the pains and labor I have bestowed upon them. . . . If I had 100 lb. laid me down for them to deprive me of them till my sight or life should be taken from me, I should not part from them.

Further, my will is that my son Benjamin Keayne, my executor, having first made choice out of my study of such books as he shall desire and think needful for his own use and reading (not to sell), whether divinity, history, or military, or any of my written sermon books excepting those four before given to the library, and also my wife [having chosen] some few for her use if she shall desire any other than those she hath already of her own—these premised, my will is that my brother Wilson and Mr. Norton, with my executor and overseers or the most of them, may view over the rest of my books and to choose from amongst them such of my divinity books and commentaries and of my written sermon books or any others of them as they shall think profitable and useful for such a library (not simply for show but properly for use), they being all English, none Latin or Greek. Then the rest, both the written and printed ones, which remains may be sold for their due worth. And though my books be not many nor very fit for such a work, being English and small books, yet after this beginning the Lord may stir up some others that will add more to them and help to carry the work on by books of more value, antiquity, use, and esteem. And [my desire is] that an inventory may be taken and kept of those books that they set apart for the library.

And because I perceive that the elders of the neighboring towns have appointed certain times in the year, chiefly in summer time once a month, to meet together to confer about ordering things in the churches according to God and debate about doubts or difficult questions that may arise in matters of religion and such like, and that they have no place to meet in but at one of our elders' houses, nor nothing to refresh themselves with but of themselves which may prove too great a burden to our elders (the meetings being so often and continuing constant) to bear of their own charge besides other burdens and inconveniences they may undergo—therefore, the room before mentioned being fitted that they may meet when they please thereat, I do will and bequeath four pounds a year to be paid out of some of my shops in Boston by quarterly payments, which may be ordered and disposed [of] as the elders shall direct or advise to provide some refreshing for them when they meet or now and then dinners as far as it will go and as [they] themselves shall be pleased to husband it. Not that I would put upon my executor the care of such provisions or of buying or dressing the meat, but that he should appoint which shop should pay them so much and then they may appoint a steward of their own to receive the pay every quarter, and then they to direct how it shall be laid out or disposed of for that end to their own content. Only I would premise this, [that] if their meeting be only in the summer and not in the winter as I conceive, then my will is that they should receive this four pounds every summer ... as that will be most convenient for their meeting.

And this gift of four pounds per anno I give for the space of ten years from the time of my death, if that meeting continue so long in that town, hoping that before then some other may be moved to step in and to add so much more to it as may serve to provide a moderate dinner for every time of their meeting so that no part of the charge of it may lie upon themselves. And when the 10 years is ended I doubt not if my son be then living here and my buildings continue as now that he would continue this gift of mine longer if that meeting continue longer and proves by experience to be much for the good and advantage of religion and the churches as is intended, and not to the hurt and prejudice of the same.

[Gifts to the Artillery Company: A Firing Platform and Butt]

And if a convenient, fair room in one of the buildings before mentioned be sequestered and set apart for an armory and the meeting of the Artillery ... (I am not strict for the very place so they have content in it, though yet I think the very heart and securest part of the town ... is the most fit for a magazine for arms because of the danger of surprising of them) the place that they now use will be fit to scour and tend the arms in, and the other to lay them up and keep them in, which will be a comely sight for strangers to see and a great ornament to the room and also to the town where the soldiers may arm themselves every time they go to exercise. Such a place being provided, I give and bequeath five pounds for the encouragement of that Company to be laid out in pikes and bandoleers for the use of such soldiers of that Company that live in other towns so far as it cannot be convenient for them to bring their arms with them. Or if the officers of that Company do know any other thing that the Company wants that will be more useful for the general good of the Company than what I have mentioned, [something] that will continue and not be spent or consumed in the use, then I am willing that the whole or any part of this legacy may be so disposed of, taking in the advice and consent of my executor in the same.

Item. I give and bequeath further to this Artillery Company of Boston five pounds more towards the erecting of a platform, planked underneath, for two mounted pieces of ordnance to stand upon, a greater and a smaller, with a shed of boards raised over it to keep them dry and preserve them from sun and weather. This [is] to be raised in the most convenient part in the training place in Boston where it shall be most fit for that use and where at a convenient distance against some hill or rising ground there may be a good butt or kind of bulwark raised of earth that may receive the shot of these pieces and may be free from endangering any that may unexpectedly pass by or be behind the butt in case they should overshoot. This butt may be cast up or digged at the bottom of a hill without any charge by the Company themselves in two or three of their training days. My end in this is that the Company may be trained up (or so many of them as desire it) in the use, exercise, and experience of the great ordnance as they are in their muskets, that they may learn how to traverse, load, mount, level, and fire at a mark, etc., which is as needful a skill for a soldier as the exercise of their ordinary arms. I suppose the country[2] will willingly lend the Company two such pieces for so good a use as this is if the town itself hath none such to spare, and will give them a barrel of powder or two to encourage them to begin a service that will be so singularly useful for the country. The bullets will be most of them found and saved again if the hill or butt against which they shoot be not so low and narrow that they overmount and shoot aside at random.

Now as many of that Company or others [as] desire to learn that art of gunnery (so needful for every captain and officer of a company to be experienced in) ... may enter their names to be scholars of the great artillery. [They are] to agree that every one that enters his name may give so much for entry and so much a year afterwards as you do at the

---

[2] I.e., the Commonwealth of Massachusetts.

Artillery. This money will serve to lay in provision of powder, shot, sponges, budge-barrels, cannon baskets, and some allowance to the master gunner that shall take pains to instruct them, if there cannot be some skillful and sufficient man found that will think the honor of the place to instruct such a society in so noble a service recompense sufficient. [For] they have an opportunity not only to exercise their own skill but to do good to the country and to willing scholars that so thirst after experience. We see the captain and the rest of the officers of the small artillery do freely expend their time to instruct others in the best skill themselves have attained, and look at it as reward enough that their pains is accepted and the Company edified by it. Besides, there are many shipmasters and gunners that resort to this country who have good skill in this art, and I doubt not [that] upon their request the Company might have their help sometimes and direction herein. He that is chosen to this place may have the title of the captain of the great artillery, or master gunner, and there may be a time appointed once in a week or fortnight for the scholars to meet and to spend two or three hours, either forenoon or afternoon, for their instruction in it. Now all that meet cannot every one expect to make a shot, for that would prove too great a charge and expense of powder. But everyone must take their turn and two or three at a meeting make one shot apiece, or but one man two shots at one time. The rest may observe as much by the manner of their performing it as if they had done it themselves.

And for further encouragement to help on this exercise besides the five pounds given before towards the platform and the other five pounds for pikes etc., I give and bequeath two heifers or cows to the captain and officers of the First Artillery Company to be kept as a stock constantly and the increase or profit of these cows yearly to be laid out in powder or bullets, etc., for the use of the exercise of the great artillery. . . . At no time [is] the stock or the value of it . . . to be diminished. These [are] to be delivered to the captain that shall have the command of that Company or whom himself and officers shall appoint when the platform and butt is finished and two pieces mounted thereon with all materials thereto belonging fit to exercise with and when a master or captain of the great ordnance is chosen, a convenient company, between ten and twenty, of soldiers entered for scholars, and all things settled in a good posture for the beginning and continuance of that exercise. But if the Artillery Company shall neglect to accomplish this before expressed above two years after my decease, then these three legacies, viz., both the five pounds and the two cows, [are] to be void and to be to the use of my executor. But if the things before mentioned be accomplished and this new company do go on as I desire it may, then my will is that the captain with the consent of the Company may appoint some able man either of the Company or otherwise that shall give bond to my executors or overseers for these two cows or the value of them at the time of delivery [so] that the stock shall be preserved and the increase or benefit of them only to be disposed of for the use of this new company. And if this company should break off and not continue their exercise, then the two cows or the just value that they were worth at the time of their first delivery [are] to be returned to my executor or some of my overseers for his use. Now any man that shall have the cows to keep [must] be willing to give such a bond if the Company order it so, in case that exercise should fall to the ground. For the two first five pounds I desire no bond nor any return of it, though the Company should not continue very long. I would make [this] my dying request to our First Artillery Company (if there shall be such a Company in being when it shall please God to take me out of this miserable world).

Many knows what my earnest endeavors and desires hath been to promote and encourage what I could since the Lord hath brought me into this country, and my desires have not been altogether frustrated. For out of this small Company the Lord hath raised up many a well experienced soldier that hath done good service and have been of good esteem both here and in our native country. And therefore my grief is the more to see that when the country grows more populous this sometime flourishing and highly prized Company should grow more thin and ready to dissolve for want of appearance. Some are weary and others think they have got experience enough, so the most begins to neglect. But my request is that the entries, quarterage, and fines for late and non-appearance (which last hath been too long neglected and will not be well with the Company till it be taken up again, especially seeing the greatest part of that Company consists now of men in our own town and we never had better nor more constant appearance than when fines were duly taken) may be preserved and kept in stock to lay out in powder, arms, bandoleers for the use of the Company, and also in canvas to make resemblance of trenches, half moons, redoubts, forts, etc., cannon baskets, and such like necessary implements for some special military service that might be performed once or twice a year. This would be a singular help to the ordinary exercise, and would add much not only to the encouragement but to the experience both of officers and soldiers in some military exercises which, without such helps as these, cannot be taught nor performed. And these moneys would be far better employed and to the greater satisfaction and content of the Company in such things than [if] wasted and spent in eating and drinking and needless invitations, as it hath been a long time both to my own and to the grief and offense of several of the Company. This hath occasioned some to leave the Company and others to be unwilling to pay their quarterage, seeing the whole stock is still consumed and the Company rather in debt than otherwise. It hath been a chief thing to hinder many other profitable exercises for want of means to bear the charge of them and will in time be the overthrow and dissolution of the Company if it be not prevented.

What hath made the Artillery Company in London so to flourish for so long a time together but the stock of the Company well managed whereby they have done great things and have been able to perform many exercises (though chargeable) both for the delight of all beholders and the great benefit and experience of the soldiers and the increase of their number? Indeed, I had in my purpose several other legacies to have bestowed on this Company for their encouragement and the example of others and have them in a readiness and of some consequence. But the small appearance of the Company and the declining of it daily which cannot be but a great discouragement to the captain and officers that command them, as also to the soldiers that do appear and causes a kind of contempt instead of esteem in those that behold them, makes me fear the final dissolution of it, and so all gifts will sink with it and come to nothing. [This] hath been the cause of altering my resolution. ... I know [that] a skillful commander, though he have a body of men but 4 files, 6 deep, which is but 24 soldiers, yea I would add further if he have but half so many, but two files, 6 or 8 deep, with them he may perform such variety of exercises, not only for the postures but the several motions, doublings, facings, counter-marches, wheelings, yea such variety of forms of battles and several kinds of firings and charges as should be not only delightful but very useful and gainful to those that are exercised, and not only for two or three training days but have matter enough to exercise them for several years. I should hardly have believed this did not I know it to be true and have seen it with mine eyes. Yet notwithstanding, what comfort or credit can a captain have to go into the field with 6 or 12 soldiers and under the name of an artillery or military company? It would be my rejoicing if there could be any means thought on or used to increase and encourage this Company that is and may be so honorably advantageous to the whole country, that it may remain and continue still in splendor and esteem, increasing and not declining. But all things have their changes.

The Apologia of Robert Keayne 15

[These Gifts Justified: No Selfish Aims]

Now concerning the original legacy of three hundred pounds that I
have given to the town of Boston for the raising of a conduit in the market place and for a building to fit for such uses as I have before mentioned, if any shall allege that three hundred pounds is not sufficient to
accomplish it I answer, 1, that it may be some of these may be gone about
and finished by the town before God may call me out of this world,
[such] as the conduit or market house etc., and then there will be the
less to do. I know that the town hath agitated it and seriously intended to
have gone about to do them all except only the library, as such things that
are needful and will turn to the public advantage of the town. 2ly, I say
that I conceive if it be well managed and ordered it may do it all or very
near it. I suppose one of the two last houses that I built hath room enough
in it to accomplish all the ends before mentioned, excepting the conduit,
if it had been first contrived and thought on for such an end. Yet that
hath not cost me 400 lb., not by so much as I suppose will near build a new
conduit. But, thirdly, if it should fall short I do expect and suppose that
the town will be willing to add to it and make up the rest either by enlarg-
ing of the conveniences or beautifying the structure for the better ornament of the town. And possibly some [one] else may think of some other
thing wanting which I have not thought upon that may be as useful to
the general good of the town as most of these, to be added to it. Besides,
if I were about to build a thing that I conceive would be very useful and
advantageous to me but am not comfortably able to bear the charge of
it, if any friend out of love to me would lend me 300 lb. [for] some
considerable time gratis it would be a great encouragement to me to go
on with the work. But if he should offer to give me freely 300 lb. towards
it I should think myself bound to be very thankful to him and to be willing
to make up what is wanting rather than [to] lose so free a kindness by
my neglecting of the work.

But possibly some will be ready to apprehend that I may do this only
for my own ends and benefit, which may make them the more backward
to have it go on, especially with any of their own cost. For some such spirits
there be that had rather deny themselves a benefit than that another
should enoy a greater benefit by it. . . . Some have said that I have been
very forward to have a conduit in that place because I have so many
houses and buildings thereabout, and so a market house will be the more
beneficial to bring trade to my shops. I answer, [suppose] that this were
in all things true, it is not sinful nor unlawful in Christian prudence to

provide means for the preventing of danger or procuring of any lawful good; I doubt not but they would do the like if it were their own case. But 2dly, what advantage will this be to me when I am dead and gone, if others should not receive more benefit than I by it? I need not trouble myself with what may fall out in after times in these respects, for I shall feel no want nor suffer any damage by such losses. A 100 things would come into consideration as needful to prevent or provide for as these if men going out of the world should trouble themselves with the care of such changes and things that may happen when they are dead. 3dly, if my houses only were there and no other shops but mine there might be more ground for such an apprehension. But it is the heart of the town and many fair buildings and shops there be round about. The market is there seated already. The market house is more for the conveniency of strangers and their accommodation in winter and summer, in wet and dry, [than] for the inhabitants of the town. And in that respect it is a work of charity and mercy, and though some particular persons that trade may have more benefit by it than some other persons that dwell further off, yet the advantage and profit of it will redound to the whole town in general. For my own particular—I having given over trade long ago— the nearness of the market is more chargeable than beneficial to me if I looked not at a general and public good more than my private.

As for the conduit, I confess it is very necessary and useful in many respects, especially in danger of fire, and well it were if there were more of them in the town than there is. But that it will be more beneficial to me or that I shall have more need of it than others, who can tell? Who knows that my house alone shall be set on fire? God may preserve mine though divers others may be consumed, as it fell out lately by sad experience. Had there been a conduit in the market place before, then would it not have been looked at and found to be a public good? Might not some of the houses been saved that were consumed worth more than the charge of setting up three or four such conduits? Nay, if the fire had gone on in its rage as it was most like (had not God in unexpected mercy prevented it) and seized upon others' houses as it threatened to do, the whole town would have had cause to have bewailed the want of it and to think that such a conduit was a public good and the want of it a public evil though some particular persons might have had the benefit of it at that time more than others, and at some other times others might have had more need and more benefit by it than they. But if my houses and shops stood alone or if I only should need and not others, if it were for my own private and not for the public good of others, I would build a conduit and a market house too if there were need at my own charge without calling in the help of others. I think, if my own heart deceive me not, my aim in all these things proposed is for the general good of the town and that if I had no house thereabouts but had lived in some other part of the town I should be as forward to promote these works as I have been formerly or am at this present. So I should desire all my loving brethren and neighbors of the town to interpret and accept of what I tender to them as a fruit of my true endeavor and desire of the town's good and not at any private advantage of me or mine, and as [from] one that have been willing and desirous to help them forward in my lifetime rather than death.

And for that legacy of one hundred pounds before mentioned for the granary to begin a stock for a public magazine of corn for the town or chiefly the poorer sort in it, now what private ends or advantage can anyone apprehend I can have in that when I am dead? And so for the library and armory and platform and butt for the encouragement of the Artillery Company or free school or what I had set apart formerly for the training up of the Indians' children in learning and some English scholars to learn the Indian tongue. Now if these cannot but be interpreted for a public and general good to the town, why should any conceive otherwise of the other? As for the conduit, there is none in the market place and if such a work be needful in any part of the town it is 5 times more needful there. And so for the market house, [unless] there were more public markets set up in some other parts of the town.

[Additional Gifts, Repaying Evil with Good, Unkindness with Kindness]

And though God hath been pleased in some measure to carry me on with a public spirit to seek the good of the town according to that ability which God hath been pleased to afford unto me (though I am not able to do according to the largeness of my desire, hoping that God will raise up some others after me of abler estates and opener hearts and hands to add larger additions to these weak beginnings or to begin some others that may be more useful than these) yet I must needs say I have met with discouragements more than a few to divert my thoughts and purposes another way and to tie up both my heart and hands from such testimonies of my love [as] I have been willing to show. [I have been discouraged] not only by these objections I have now answered, but by those unkind and unneighborly discourtesies that I have more lately and formerly met withal in this town. . . . These I cannot easily forget, though I desire to forgive. [They came] from many in the church, especially in those times of my troubles, and more their spirits and dispositions would have led them to had not the providence of God and the tenderness and wisdom of some others amongst us prevented their desires and endeavors. Their actions and proceedings I could never take as a fruit of their love to my soul as much as a fruit of their prejudice against my person. But I desire to requite their evil with good and unkindness with kindness.

Therefore, my will about the ordering of this 100 lb. to be paid in corn, cattle, or a part in both [is] that it may be preserved still for a stock from year to year, and the increase or profit of it to be disposed of only for the uses intended, which are these that follow. The one half hereof, viz., fifty pounds with the increase thereof, I give and bequeath to the use of the free school at Boston to help on the training up of some poor men's children of Boston (that are most towardly and hopeful) in the knowledge of God and of learning, not only in the Latin tongue but also [in] writing and ciphering as far as the profit of it will reach and according to the best ordering of it for that end as the townsmen or feoffees of the free school from time to time shall judge best, taking in also the advice of my executor or executors with my overseers or the most part of them so long as they live or as any of them remain in the country. The other fifty pounds with the profit of it I give and bequeath for the use and relief of the poor members of our own church or to any other good use that shall be accounted as necessary or more necessary than this that I intend ... in the judgment of all the elders and deacons of this our church from time to time, with the consent of my executor and overseers as before.

Now if that school should be sufficiently provided for before I die, then I would propound it to be kept as a magazine of store from year to year and as a stock for the town if either a famine or war should happen amongst us, which may tend much for the preservation of the town especially for the poorer sort. 400 bushels of Indian [corn] may be bought for 50 lb. and 250 if not 300 bushels of rye and also peas for 50 lb. How easy a thing it would be for the town to make it up a 1000 bushels or more by every family putting in but a peck of corn or such a matter but once in a year or but once in all to raise a first stock, to sell it away once in two years or longer if it will keep when it bears the best price and lay it in again when it may be cheapest bought, which will bear the charge of waste and looking to with considerable profit. It may be expended yearly for some of the most necessary and charitable uses of the town. Much good may be done by it and the stock still not diminished but aug-

mented. Or if the whole 100 lb. were put into a stock of corn and so hus-
banded constantly, and the one-half of the profit go to the disposing of
the church and the other to the town I perceive no inconvenience in it.
This hath been the wisdom and care of our forefathers in other parts,
and much public good have been done by it. I know not why we should
not imitate them herein [unless] some other way may be thought of
wherein such a stock may be employed with less trouble and more certain
profit and yet accomplish the main ends I intend herein, the relief of the
godly poor. As far as the profits of it may run, I should willingly give
way to it.

And because my will and earnest desire is that this stock of 100 lb.
might be constantly preserved for the uses above said (except God should
take it away by fire or some such extraordinary accident or special hand
of God, in [which] case I should earnestly beg of the town to make it up
again—which may be done without any great burden to them and they
are like to reap the benefit of it in the mean time) I propose this as necessary and by me desired, that security may be given to my executor or
overseers for this 100 lb. at the receiving of it by some of the townsmen
and to repay it again in case they do not preserve it and constantly improve
it to the uses before mentioned or some other that may be better or equiva-
lent to it according to my true intent and meaning therein, which is to do
the most and best good with it that it may be employed to. And lest the
townsmen should object that they are changeable every year and so may
refuse to give bond, though it be for a public good, then I think the deacons who are usually [chosen] for their lives or . . . some feoffees chosen
for that end may give bond for it and they to have the whole 100 lb. to
improve for the uses before. However, I doubt not but several ways may
be thought on to secure it without any damage to one or two in particular, which I leave to the townsmen and deacons to consult and conclude
of. In the meantime I [recall to] them [that] in these two last years I
have gained for the poor seventeen pounds more than I have given away,
which is to be added to the former hundred pounds. And because I have
been fain to borrow of this poor's stock for my own use when I have wanted money of my own, and it hath been a good help and supply to me that
way many times, therefore I am willing to make the seventeen pounds
twenty pounds as I have formerly done upon the same ground. When
their stock was but eighty and odd pounds I made it up [to] one hundred
pounds. Therefore, whatsoever there shall be wanting in ready cash in
the poor's stock of one hundred and twenty pounds my will and order to
my executor or executors is that they may make it up out of my own es-

tate in current pay answerable to money and to be more careful in it than in the discharge of any other debt that I shall then owe.

[*Profitable Management of the Poor Fund Justified*]

Now for this 120 lb. before mentioned, I am bound to acknowledge and to leave this testimony behind me concerning it and how I came by it. For I do not account it properly my own nor simply my gift to the poor now but their due and debt as that which for these many years, long before I came out of Old England, I began to gather and devote ... to God and his service for such a particular use now mentioned what of it I could save and spare besides what I yearly gave away out of it to pious uses as necessity called for at my hands, both in Old England and since I came hither. This stock I have gathered and from week to week laid apart by taking one penny out of every shilling which I have gotten by my trade, with other goods and merchandise that I have dealt in. So that when I gained much in a week there hath been the more laid aside for any good use and when trading hath been dead and the gains less, there hath been the less laid aside for this stock and use. This course I have constantly kept above this 40 years. And I now mention this the more particularly not in any way of boasting for any good work that I have either done or can do (for I know if God should enter into judgment with me for any or the best of them all He might justly reject both me and them as abominable), but that all that know it or may hear of it may take notice of the blessing of God upon such a free and voluntary course. Some others when they know it maybe will be willing to imitate and bless God for it, as some in Old England have done to their great content and satisfaction.

By this means I have had commonly lying by me 50 lb., 60 lb., or 80 lb. ready money especially in Old England and some pretty quantity here, till more lately since money hath been so scarce amongst us, whereby I have been fain to borrow out of that stock myself for my own necessary use and occasions when I have wanted money of my own. And a good comfortable help it hath been to me that way in many pinches. But [I] still do keep a careful account [of] what at any time I take out, and [I] pay it in again as money comes to hand. Out of this stock usually lying by me I have had opportunity to lend to any poor godly Christian or minister in need (besides what I give away) 40 s., 5 lb., or a greater sum to help them in a strait, and to make use of it in their trades for a convenient time. [These loans] have done some more good than if they had at another time so much given them. Sometimes I have ventured part of it to sea, that the benefit of it might redound to the stock for the poor's use, by which means also I could more readily and willingly give away twenty shillings or five pounds at a time upon any motion to a charitable use if the occasion hath been weighty than either myself or some other good men of better estates could part with so many shillings, had it not been for such a stock in a readiness.

It is true that since I have given over trading in this country and since the way of trade is not so much for ready money as for exchange, as for corn, cattle, and other commodities, I cannot lay aside weekly as I used to do formerly. Therefore, by casting up my estate, which commonly I do once every year, I can see what I am increased in my estate, and accordingly I do lay aside yearly answerable to what I get in the whole.

Unto this stock of the poor I am indebted at this time, being mo. 6: 12: 1653, one hundred pounds sterling or 101 lb. as near as I can guess, besides all the money that is now in cash in 2 private boxes that are within my cabinet in my closet at Boston. The papers within each box will show there is as I remember ten pounds in New England money with some Old England silver and somewhat more than ten pounds in the other secret box, in which is two ten shillings pieces of Barbary gold and 258 single two pences, pence, and halfpence. These boxes are to be unlocked or opened with any ordinary pin or needle thrust into a small pinhole that is there against a piece of steel which easily will give back. [I] have formerly added to the whole stock of my own 17 or 18 lb. and now three pounds more, which is 20 or 21 lb. in all, to make up the whole stock [of] 120 lb., which I give as the poor's use for that help and supply I have received from it in the times of my own need.

Now for this money I have nothing to do but to take care that it be well paid in within one year or two at the most after my decease, if my executor cannot with conveniency pay it in before, and to provide by the best way I can suggest or devise that it be also well disposed of, improved, and employed (according to my own purpose, intent, and desire in saving it together) [so] that the stock may still remain and the profit of it yearly employed so as it may do good to many [for] as many years after my death and more as it hath done in the time of my life. Now what my way and thoughts are for the best improvement of it I have before proposed. If a more useful and profitable way can be found out both for the preserving of the stock and augmenting the profit of it I shall freely leave it to the advice of my executor and overseers, with our elders, deacons, and townsmen that shall then be, or any other that can give better advice or propose a better way. But if the townsmen, deacons, or some other by their orders shall refuse to give sufficient bond for this hundred and twenty pounds to secure the stock, then this my gift shall cease and become utterly void in respect of Boston; and I will and bequeath the said one hundred and twenty pounds to the use of Harvard College in Cambridge to be improved as I shall hereafter mention, they taking care to secure the stock.

[*Harvard College as Secondary Legatee*][3]

And for the three hundred pounds which I have given to the town of Boston to build a conduit, a market house, and town house with a library, granary, and armory, as I have before mentioned, if the town of Boston shall slight or undervalue this gift or my good will to them therein and shall refuse or neglect to go about and finish these several buildings in manner and time before mentioned rather than they will be troubled with it or add anything of their own for the finishing of it, then my will is that this gift of 300 lb. given to Boston for the uses of those buildings before mentioned shall utterly cease and become void in respect of Boston, and those gifts that I have given with relation to those buildings, as my books to the library, etc., or any others of them that I have not before provided for and ordered, shall be and remain to the sole use of the College at Cambridge in the same manner that I have ordered the former 120 lb. in corn for the poor in Boston in case the deacons or town shall refuse or neglect to give security for the principal stock, as before is mentioned.

My true meaning herein is this, that if the town of Boston shall set upon one or two of these works and neglect or refuse to carry on the rest (or some of the other that I have mentioned happily being done by the town before I die) as [for example,] if they should build only the conduit and market house and not a town house or library and gallery, or a granary and armory and not a conduit or market house, etc., then my will is that my executor shall give only such a proportion of this three hundred pounds as that work or building shall come to. [This proportion] they [shall] set upon only in relation to this gift of mine compared with the value of the other buildings that I have likewise mentioned [which] they have left undone. ... What upon that account shall be

---

[3] The early results of Keayne's benefaction to Harvard may be conveniently traced in the Harvard College Records (these *Publications*, xv, xvi). The income from the bequest is still being paid towards beneficiary aid to "the godliest and most hopefulest of the poorer sort of scholars." See, *Official Register of Harvard University*, LIII, no. 18 (September, 1956), 8.

reserved of the 300 lb. shall be for the use of the College of Cambridge, [to which] I have given the whole 300 lb. in case they refuse or neglect to finish all those buildings or any of them within two or three years after my death, as before I have ordered.

Now if the 120 lb. and this 300 lb. or any part thereof shall fall to the College, my desire is that it should be improved not about the buildings or repairs of the College, for that I think the country should do and look after, but for the use and help of such poor and hopeful scholars whose parents are not comfortably able to maintain them there for their diet and learning, or for some addition yearly to the poorer sort of fellows or tutors whose parents are not able nor themselves have not ability nor supplies otherwise to defray their charge and make their studies comfortable. My true intent herein, so that it may easily be discerned, is not that one or two should enjoy the benefit of it all or but for a year or two, but according to the proportion of that sum which shall fall to the College my desire is that the godliest and most hopefulest of the poorer sort of scholars may have an addition to that which their parents allows them, of 20 or 40 s. a year apiece while they abide in the College or till some providence may help their supplies otherwise, or that as far as it will extend some may have the help of it for 2 or 3 years and then others may have the help and comfort of it 2 or 3 years after, and so in order as long as the benefit of this gift may continue. [Perhaps] it may prove more useful to dispose of it for an addition or an enlargement to the commons of the poorer sort of scholars, which I have often heard is too short and bare for them.

Therefore, because I have little insight in the true ordering of scholars and other things thereto belonging in a college way and so possibly may dispose of my gift where there is less need and that it may do more good if it had been employed in some other way, I am willing to refer it to the President, Feoffees, and Overseers that are entrusted with the care and ordering of the College and scholars or students with the things thereto belonging, still taking in the consent of my executor and of such of the overseers of this my will as shall then be alive. What they together shall judge to be the best and most needfulest way of employing of it amongst the scholars I shall consent to. And when the certain sum is known that doth fall to the College, the President and Overseers may confer with my executor and overseers and . . . cast up what such a sum would purchase by the year for 20 years, or a longer time, and if they agree and my executor consent to it he may keep the legacy in his own hands and pay to the College yearly for so long a time as they agree upon so much per annum out of some part of my lands or houses as they shall set apart for that end. I do not enjoin it but only propose it and leave it to the will and consent of my executor as he shall think with the advice of my overseers will be most convenient for him, though I like best . . . paying of it yearly, if there should not appear some great inconvenience to other parts of my land to have any part of it engaged so long together for the payment of such a rent. . . . I think that some one house or shop may be appointed for such an end and some such way may be thought of as may prove no inconvenience to my executor or his estate more than to pay it out to the College and to leave them to purchase with it somewhere else. For my will and desire is in this as it is in my former legacies that the stock may be preserved by purchasing therewith something to the College, and the benefit or profit thereof to be yearly distributed as far as it will go to the most necessary uses, as I have before expressed.

And concerning my books that I have given to begin the library withal in Boston, my will is that my brother Wilson and Mr. Norton, elder at Boston, or the teaching elders that shall at the time of my death (after my wife and son Benjamin have made choice of some books for their own use, as I have before expressed) may be requested to take pains to view over the rest of my books and to take a particular note or inventory of such as they shall judge fit for that use and so to take them into their own keeping or to leave them with my executor if they will till the time mentioned in this will be accomplished, [so] that if the town of Boston should not within three years after my death build a handsome room for a library and another for the elders and scholars to walk and meet in, as before I have expressed, that then they may be delivered to the President or some of the Overseers of Harvard College in Cambridge to be placed as my gift or addition to that library that is already begun there.

[Gifts for Indian Education Withdrawn: Mr. Eliot's Unkind Carriage]

I had in some of my former wills set apart some legacies for the training up of some of the Indians, as also of their children, to be taught to write and read and to learn the English tongue, and had thought upon and proposed some ways how to get . . . their children and youth that they might be so taught, and also that some of our scholars or young students might be encouraged to study and learn the Indian tongue exactly and they then to be set apart to confer with, to catechize, and instruct the Indians in the grounds and principles of religion and to preach or prophesy to them in their own language, as they should have been ordered and directed either by the magistrates or elders or both. I had also left some pledge of my love and respect to Mr. Eliot and some others that have taken pains to instruct and teach the Indians in the ways of God. But the truth is that unkind carriage of Mr. Eliot (that I may put no worse title upon it) in seeking to interrupt, yea to take away not only from myself but from some others also certain farms, not given to us by the General Court but my own, bought with my money of the worship my brother Dudley and some others, [has dissuaded me]. After [the land] was granted by the Court to be in that place and after I had been at the charge to survey it, measure it, bound it, mark it, and lay it out, and after it was again ratified and confirmed to me by the General Court, ... I was informed by more than two or three that he would not be taken off nor persuaded by any, nay by none that spake with him about it, to surcease his prosecution or endeavor to pluck it out of our hands again for the Indians though there was land enough granted to them by the General Court without the bounds of any of our farms.

This carriage of his would have much straitened my resolutions in what I had set apart for this great work though no further help had come in for the carrying of it on, the action itself being very unsavory and offensive not only to ourselves but to many others if not to the most that had heard of it, though they were not concerned in it as we were. Therefore, I would make it my request to the reverend elders of this country not to be too stiff and resolute in accomplishing their own wills and ways, but to hearken to the advice and counsel of their brethren and to be as easily persuaded to yield in civil and earthly respects and things as they expect to prevail with any of us when they have a request to make to us for one thing or another, lest by too much stiffness to have their own wills and way they hinder many good works that may be profitable to themselves and to the whole country. But God hath been pleased to provide such a comfortable supply from larger and fuller purses to carry on this great and good work amongst the Indians and fully to recompense all that labor and take pains about it, that they shall not need the help of particular persons to make any addition that way.

Now concerning the College at Cambridge, because there is some doubt or uncertainty in it whether the whole three hundred pounds or the four hundred and twenty pounds before mentioned or any part of it will come to the use of the College, it depending upon the will and action of the church and town of Boston to accept or refuse it upon the terms before mentioned, therefore, if none of it or anything under the one-half

of the whole sum, which is two hundred and ten pounds, shall fall to the
College, then I give and bequeath one hundred pounds of that which I
had formerly set apart for the Indians to be now to the use of the College.
This 100 lb. will purchase twenty cows, and those cows will be let for
twenty pounds a year, and the stock still preserved by a careful ordering
of them. This twenty pounds per anno I desire may be distributed and
disposed of to the best good of the scholars as I have before proposed. But
if the whole 420 lb. or the one-half of it should come to the College,
then my will is that this last legacy of one hundred pounds shall become
void or otherwise to stand firm and be made good unto them after the
three years time allowed to the town of Boston, [during] which it will
be discovered whether all or any part of the former sum will come unto
them, is ended.

[*Tardiness in Giving, Defended*]

If any shall wonder or demand why I have let alone all these gifts and
good deeds mentioned in this will till I die and have not done somewhat in my lifetime, though not so much, when I might have seen the
disposing of it myself and have helped to have set them on foot and to
have settled and made a beginning in them and so have reaped the benefit of the prayers of the poor and the comfort of such good acts while I
had lived, I answer, the prayers of the faithful is much to be desired and
prized—to have the loins and backs and bellies of the poor to bless a man
while he lives is a comfortable thing. But that must be obtained in a lawful and well-regulated way, lest while some have occasion to bless others
may take occasion to curse or reproach.

If, indeed, I had given nothing or but very little in my lifetime to any
good work or to relieve the necessity of the straits or had done little or
no good with that estate which God hath bestowed upon me, then it
might have been cast upon me as a reproach. But . . . I have endeavored
to honor God with my substance and with the first fruits of all my increase, and have endeavored to do good with what God hath bestowed
upon me so far as I might likewise provide for the necessities of my own
family, the care of carrying on my calling, and other dealings in the
world justly. A man is best able himself to judge what he can do or what
he can spare to this or that good work better than others that know not
his charge, straits, or occasions. It is an easy matter for others to carve
large portions out of others men's estates and tell what they might or
should do. Yet he may do as much as his estate will permit comfortably
or as God requires at his hands, though all men do neither see it nor

know it nor all that are in need and deserve supply cannot taste of it. Neither do I think that God doth require a man to be so liberal in his life (except urgent necessity calls for it at his hands) as thereby to cast his own family into straits or wants or that shall disenable him comfortably to discharge his own debts or engagements or to carry through the care and charge of his family. Then there is no just cause of censure. God doth not require that others should be eased and we grieved. But some have a special faculty to censure other men's actions and direct what others should do or might do when they see not their own defects or neglects, and to extol and multiply small acts of their own and undervalue greater in others because they know them not, as if themselves could not have praise but by dispraising and censuring of others.

I answer that time past, present, and to come are all one with God. He takes notice of the purpose and intents of the heart. If it be real he is pleased to accept of the will for the deed and of good actions intended to be done as if they were already done, when there is just cause to hinder or prolong them. David had a good desire and purpose to build God a house in his lifetime, but his providing and preparing that it might be built after his death was accepted, yea better accepted, of God than if he had done it in his life. If a man did look after outward applause and the praise of men more than of God it were a great inducement to do all while he lived and nothing when he died. But doubtless good works provided for in a man's life but not known till after his death, if they be free from superstition and an opinion of merit, is most free from ambition and popular applause.

I answer [further,] when that uncomfortable trouble and censure passed upon me in the Court I was indebted near or altogether thirty hundred pounds, which was sufficient to have broken the back of any one man in the country, though he had been of a better estate than myself. So [it] would have [happened to] me if God had not carried me through it beyond my own expectation or foresight. Now my care (and according to my duty if I mistake not) hath been, first, to pay these debts, that every man might have his due honestly and without trouble or just complaint, and withal to provide for my family, which hath not been small nor carried on with a light or easy charge and yet with no more prodigality than what necessity and wise Providence hath called for at my hands. Considering also the great losses that I have had by sea and land, had I been wanting in care for the discharge of either of these I should have born the burden and reproach with little support or comfort from the country. I must have stood upon my own legs or fallen into greater straits in respect of men whatsoever my public good works or bounty to others might have been. In such a case they would not have been so well esteemed but rather taken as fruits of my folly, prodigality, or vainglory. I would not have wanted for variety of censures, according to several men's fancies and affections. But I have now got comfortably through or near [through] all those great debts and charges that I have been at so that I begin but now to breathe as it were, and through the great mercy and unexpected support and assistance of my good God to stand upon my own legs, and do but now as it were learn to go alone. I was not in a capacity to do it before, though God was pleased to give me a comfortable estate. But as soon as the Lord was pleased to carry me through my engagements, then God put it into my mind to think what I might do in acknowledging my thankfulness towards Him, not only in words but in some real actions or deeds. This purpose of mine I hope He will accept of not according to what I have not, but according to what I have (though it could not conveniently be before but after my death). And how few my days on this earth may be He alone knoweth, and it is in His hands alone to make good these my poor intentions and desires by preserving what now He hath of His goodness given to me, or by increasing of it through His blessing while I live. And these are the true reasons why I durst not adventure before upon such works as these: not for want of affection or desire but for want of convenient opportunity and ability to do it.

[Additional Gifts: To His Son His Own Religious Writings, More Precious Than Gold]

Item. I give and bequeath to my loving son, Major Benjamin Keayne, over and above the third part of my clear estate, both of lands, goods, and debts, etc., as before mentioned and intended, the great gold emerald ring that was my wife's father's and [is] now in my wife's keeping. I desire that he may keep it by him and neither sell nor give away as long as he lives, except some great necessity should force him thereunto.

Item. I give and bequeath to him, further, as my special gift to him my little written book in my closet upon 1 Cor. 11, 27, 28, which is a treatise on the sacrament of the Lord's Supper per Mr. Briarly. [It is] a little thin pocket book bound in leather, all written with my own hand, which I esteem more precious than gold, and which I have read over I think 100 and 100 times. I hope he will read it over no less [and will] make it his constant companion, and that it may be as precious to him as ever it was and as still it is to me. I would not have him deny anyone that desires [to] have a copy of it, but I desire him and hope that he will never part with it as long as he lives.

I must acknowledge that in some of my former wills I did by special gift bequeath to him likewise my 3 great written paper books upon the exposition of the Bible upon this expectation and request that he would carry on the same work in manner as I have began, which will be a work of his whole life. But I have considered since that he will be hardly able, nor it may be willing, to take so much pains and . . . also that such a work as that, which may be so beneficial and useful to a society of men (except for the end before mentioned) and is more fit for public than private uses and more useful for scholars than others, should [not] be appropriated to one man only. Considering further that I have given liberty to my son to make choice of some books out of my study such as he shall find most useful and necessary for his own study and reading, both divinity and history, therefore, I have since thought it would be more useful to give them to some public library, as now I have done. And I would add only this, that when I am dead, upon the perusal of my study there will be found many books both printed and written (which I have read over) that have divers leaves turned down thick in them. They are only such choice places which I intended, and was a part of my constant work while I lived, so far as they concern scripture and exposition, to transcribe into those 4 great paper books before mentioned. . . . I have generally done [the same] by all the books that I have and do read, and should be glad if some ingenious young scholar that hath a good, legible hand and a ready and willing mind that delights in writing and reading were requested to carry it on till the work come to be more nearly finished.

*[Additional Gifts: To His Wife
A Silver Bowl and the Second-Best Bed]*

Item. I give and bequeath to my loving wife, Mrs. Anne Keayne, over and above her third part of my lands and houses, the benefit and profit whereof she is to have during her natural life . . . and besides those books that she commonly makes use of for her own reading, and besides her own wearing apparel of all sorts, I give and bequeath to my said wife one feather bed and bedstead with a feather bolster and one pillow, two white blankets, one rug, two pair of sheets, two pillowbears, with a pair of curtains and valence suitable to her own use, not the best of all that I have in my house but the . . . second or next to the best of all, if there should be any material difference between them.

Item. I give and bequeath more as a further token of my love to her that great silver beer bowl that was given to us both by Mr. Prescott at the time of his death. (I mean he gave us 3 lb. to buy a piece of plate, with which and some additions of my own money put to it I bought this cup, which engraven upon the bowl thereof to be the gift of Mr. Prescott to us.) Now because I know that I shall leave (God being pleased to bless and prosper that estate which now I have) a comfortable estate both to my wife and son . . . and because I have already given to my son Benjamin Keayne a comfortable portion at his marriage, which is all that he can challenge, by agreement between my brother Dudley, myself, and son at the consummation of that unhappy and uncomfortable match between them[4]—therefore, I hope my son will not think [ill] of what I do here give away by legacies out of my own estate or out of my own third part, but will be studious to perform them according to my true intent, I having besides what is before mentioned showed both my care and love in leaving him a comfortable estate again by what I now leave or give to him.

[The Just Appraisal of the Estate]

And because I know I have not money to pay my several gifts or legacies bequeathed in this will, my whole estate lying chiefly in land and housing, with some debts, cattle, corn, household stuff, plate, and divers sorts of tools and movables for carting, plowing, and that these legacies will lie chiefly upon my heir and executor to see discharged and performed, and as I would not wrong my executor by paying out the chief and most vendible estate in legacies, leaving the worst thereof to him for his portion, or by forcing him to sell off all the cattle or stock of my farm to pay legacies and so to hurt or overthrow the farm and the profit thereof for want of a stock to let out with it, so on the other side I would not have my legacies stopped unpaid or by any means diverted from their proper uses intended upon any pretense of having overgiven my estate or more than I have left to discharge it with, [unless] some manifest declension in my present estate (by fire, death of cattle, or the plunder of some enemy or some great change of the times or government which

[4] Benjamin Keayne married Sarah, daughter of Governor Thomas Dudley. It soon developed that she was given to certain excessive enthusiasms. She was banished from the First Church on 24 October 1647, not only for "irregular prophecying," but also for "falling into odious, lewd, and scandalous unclean behavior with one Nicholas Hart, an excommunicated person of Taunton." *The Records of the First Church of Boston* (These *Publications*, XXXIX), 49. For other details, see *Suffolk Deeds* (Boston, 1880–1906), I. 83, 84.

should much alter the price and value of houses, land, cattle, and other goods from the common worth and estimate of things as they are now) should plainly appear. In such cases it is just and equal that the legacies should bear a proportionable loss or abatement, as well as that other part of my estate which I have bequeathed to my wife and son. Only that one hundred and twenty pounds given to the poor of the poor's stock and such particular gifts in plate or household by special name mentioned, as to my wife and son, excepted, [are to be] paid fully as my debt.

Therefore, that all things may be carried on equally and honestly, my will and desire is that the rest of my whole estate may be appraised and justly and equally valued, not underfoot but to their proper worth and value, by some men of honesty that are skillful and understanding in the several sorts and kinds of goods or lands that is to be valued according to their best judgments and apprehensions, as I have before ordered. And these appraisers [are] to be ... informed by my executor or overseers before they go about it what my will and desire is herein. This done and the value cast up, my son, having not only a third part in my land but also of my goods, cattle, and the rest of my estate, he may make choice of such part of the household stuff, cattle, or other goods as he desires, amounting to a third part of them, at the prices they are valued at. If he will have so much in goods and if he would have more or some other particular things of the goods above his part mentioned by will, then he [is] to pay as much for it as any other would do to have the same. So also if my wife should desire any part or particular thing of the household stuff or goods or rings or piece of plate for her own use besides what I have given to her, she [is] to have it before any other, she giving the full value and as much as any other would give for the same things without fraud and not to take them at their own prices or at half the worth without being accountable to the estate for it.

This done and the stock for the farm preserved what it may, the rest of the goods and household stuff and all other things that can be spared [are] to be sold to the best advantage. ... The legacies [are to be paid] with it as far as it will go or [as far as] the legatees will be willing, if they be made acquainted with it, yea, and choose to take their legacies out of such household stuff and goods as you would sell and part withal; and so likewise for the overplus of the cattle. And if these things and my debts will not discharge all my legacies, then some part of my housing or land must be sold or engaged or set apart to make them good. Only I conceive it is best for my son to keep his inheritance whole and to part with the more goods, cattle, household stuff, debts, books, or what else may better be spared to pay legacies than quite to sell away the most part of the land or housing. This I leave to his own best consideration and to the advice and counsel of my overseers of this will, [who] I doubt not will advise him and help him by their counsel to do that which shall be most comfortable for his well-being, especially seeing [that] I have given him some considerable time for the paying of the legacies, that I might not put him upon straits to pay all on a sudden, though I think it will be his wisdom to pay them, especially the smaller gifts, as fast as he can, by degrees, as debts or pay comes in, though somewhat before the time mentioned.

And my motion about my son's keeping his lands and inheritance rather than goods is because my desire is that he would resolve to live here in this country and here to settle his abode so long as he can enjoy his peace and keep a good conscience and live comfortably, which I think he may do as well if not better than in any other part of the world that I know of, [unless] the times should much alter. Here he will have a comfortable estate to live upon without any great pains or distraction and if he should have an intent to remove himself into England to accomplish that he will be forced to sell his land it may be for half the value of it. Therefore my desire is that he would resolve to live here where he may enjoy God and His ordinances in peace, and do good in his place and help to carry on the work of God here, [unless] some impulsive and unexpected occasion should call him away, such as the overseers or the godly elders should judge to be a call of God, to carry him away. In such cases I would not so much as in my mind or desire be found a fighter against God or His will for any ends of my own.

[Gifts to His Granddaughter, for Her Christian Education]

Item. I give and bequeath to Hannah Keayne, my son Benjamin's daughter, my grandchild, three hundred pounds for a legacy, to be paid to her on the day of her marriage or at the age of twenty years, which of them shall first happen, so [long as] her marriage be not before the eighteenth year of her age. And in the meantime my will is that within two years after my death this stock or legacy may be put forth upon good security to the best advantage and improvement that it may (during the times before mentioned) in such a way as it may be best and safest to employ it in, [unless] my son Benjamin desire to keep it in his own hands upon the terms before and after mentioned, which I should like well of, he agreeing with my overseers what to allow yearly for it while he keeps it in his hands and giving security to them on his daughter's behalf for the whole. The disposing and ordering of this 300 lb. I leave to the counsel and care of my executor, her father, with the overseers, and also with the advice of her grandmother, not only how the stock may best be ordered but how she may best be educated and brought up in the fear of God and learning. The profit of this money yearly may be for her diet, clothes, and learning (a part of which my desire is may be to teach her to write well and to cipher in a reasonable manner; and if I thought she would not addict herself to it or that her father or grandmother should neglect to have her taught therein I would take away a good part of this legacy given to her) till she come to receive it herself as above said. What can be yearly spared out of the produce and profit of the stock [is] to be reserved for the increase of the main stock. I would have given more to her but that I know her father will have a good estate and, having yet no other child but she, will be able to give her more than she will deserve, besides what the love and tender affection of her grandmother will lead her to. However, if neither of them should do more for her, this of itself through God's blessing will be a comfortable portion for her maintenance, if she be not cast away in her match and if God be pleased to bring her to that estate. And my request and desire both to her father and grandmother and also my overseers [is] that all care may be taken not only for her good education but also for her marriage, that she miscarry not that way but may be bestowed of some man truly fearing God and of good esteem and report of such as do fear Him. And my special charge to her is (and it should and will be of weight to her if the fear of God be placed in her heart) that she would not dare to set her affections upon any in that kind without their advice, counsel, and help, viz., her father, grandmother, etc., in such a choice.[5]

Now if it should please God that Hannah should die before the age of twenty years unmarried or before eighteen years married, then if my son Benjamin Keayne should have any other child or children of his own lawfully begotten and living at the death of Hannah, if he have but one then I give two hundred of that 300 lb. to that one; if two, then they to have the 300 lb. between them; if three, then they to have one hundred pounds apiece, to be paid to them when either of them shall be married and upon the same terms as it was given to Hannah Keayne as above. If my son

---

[5] Keayne's concern about his granddaughter's romantic disposition and his repeated insistence that her judgment be checked by wiser heads were only too well taken. For the fantastic story of her marriages, see Morgan, "A Boston Heiress," these *Publications*, XXXIV. 499–513.

have but one child, then the odd hundred pounds I give to himself and the other 200 lb. to his child as before. But if it should please God to take Hannah away before she comes to enjoy her portion and my son have no other child, I give Hannah liberty to dispose of 10 or twenty pounds of this portion in legacies to her friends. If she should die but a year before she should receive it, then I give the whole three hundred pounds as followeth: namely, one hundred pounds thereof to my loving wife, Mrs. Anne Keayne, if she be living at the time of Hannah's death, and the other two hundred pounds unto my son Benjamin, her father, if he survive her. And if my wife should be dead before her grandchild comes to age, that hundred pounds that I give to her I give to the College at Cambridge in New England, and if God should so order it as to take away the life of my son before his daughter Hannah die and he leaves no issue behind him and [if] Hannah should die before she comes to receive her portion as before, then likewise I give and bequeath the two hundred pounds that my son should have had unto Harvard College in New England to [be] disposed of as I have formerly made mention of, with all the profits and benefits of it [except] what of it hath been expended upon Hannah before her death or at her burial. If Hannah should die but a little before she comes to age, as a year or the like, I give her liberty to dispose of ten or twenty pounds of her portion to gratify any of her friends in legacies if she desire so to do.

[*Provision for the Unexpected, and Some Minor Gifts*]

And because my son, Major Benjamin Keayne, is now in Old England and I am here and [he] may die himself before me, though we should not suddenly hear of it, or may be taken away before or in his coming hither or without making any will in relation to my estate, he not hearing or knowing what I have left him or done for him, and therefore by will hath not disposed of any part of my estate at or before his death, in such a case or cases if God should so dispose of things then my will is that his third part of my whole estate which I have given and bequeathed to him with all the benefit of any other part of my estate which shall accrue to him by virtue of his executorship (with the three hundred pounds given to his daughter Hannah, a part of which I have given to himself in case she should die before she be of that age mentioned before in this will)—if he should die before he comes to enjoy that and leave no other children lawfully begotten of his own body to inherit or possess the same, which if he have then they are to enjoy his part as I shall after mention, but in failure thereof then I dispose of it in manner following.

Imprimis, if my son should die in debt justly to any man or men that can legally or honestly make it appear to be so and was not paid or discharged before his death or the enjoying of this estate of mine left to him, then my will is that such debts of his out of this estate of mine given to him may be duly and honestly paid and discharged.

Secondly, that if my estate should fall short in anything as not sufficient to perform all my gifts and legacies mentioned in this will according to my true intent and meaning, then my will is that any such defect shall be made up and made good out of the part of my estate given to my son in case he should die before he comes to enjoy and possess it and make no will to dispose of it, or not of so much as by virtue of my will he should have enjoyed if he had lived. These two things premised ([that is,] if he should be in debt and have not sufficient out of his own peculiar estate to pay them and all my own legacies given in this will made good out of it—if there should not be estate enough of my own undisposed of remaining to do it, as I apprehend and hope there will with a comfortable remaining part left to my son's third part—) . . . then I dispose of the whole, or of what part of it that shall remain, as followeth.

Imprimis, to his daughter and my grandchild Hannah Keayne, four hundred pounds of it, upon the same terms as I have given to her the three hundred pounds before mentioned. And in case Hannah should die before she comes to enjoy this, then it [is] to be disposed of as the former to one of my son Benjamin's children, or if he should have more children than one, then to have it equally divided amongst them, as before mentioned.

If my son Benjamin Keayne should have any other child or children living at the time of his decease besides Hannah Keayne, if it be one son or more, then his eldest son to have one-half of the remaining part of his father's portion and the rest of it that remains [is] to be equally divided amongst his other children, Hannah Keayne also having a proportionable part in this also. If he have not above two children more living then besides herself, though it be by another wife than her mother, if he should have but one son and no other daughters but Hannah, then that son [is] to have one-half of his father's portion, as I said before. If he should have no son and yet have one or more daughters besides Hannah, then the one-half of what I have given to my son is to be divided between them proportionably, as I have mentioned before, and it [is] to be sequestered upon good security, that they may enjoy it when they come to age. The profit that shall arise out of their several portions [is] to be employed for their food and raiment and for their good and careful education in the fear of God and such learning as is needful for them to be trained up in. But if it should please God that my son should have no other child living at his death but Hannah Keayne and he die before he knows what I have given to him and so hath not disposed of it by his own will, as I before mentioned, then my will is that Hannah Keayne should have two hundred pounds more out of her father's part, that is six hundred pounds in all, besides the three hundred pounds that I have given to her of my own.

My will is that my loving wife Mrs. Anne Keayne, his mother, should have one hundred pounds out of that part I have left to my son in case she be then alive.

I give and bequeath to every one of my overseers mentioned in this will that shall then be alive and remaining in this country, out of my son's part ten pounds apiece for their care and pains taken and to be taken in the discharge of that trust and confidence that I put in them all, to do their uttermost to see this my will fulfilled and taking order to the uttermost of their power and skill that it may faithfully be observed and performed according to my true intent and purpose therein.

I give and bequeath out of my son's part in the cases before mentioned unto my sister Grace Jupe her three children, of whom I have yet the care of, viz., Anthony Jupe, my cousin Mary Jupe, now Mary Morse, and Benjamin Jupe, that now lives in my house, one hundred pounds to be equally divided between them. And if either of them should die before they come to enjoy it, then the other two to have fifty pounds apiece. And if but one of them remain, then that one [is] to have the whole hundred pounds.

Item. I give and bequeath out of my son's part in cases before mentioned further to my loving brother and sister Wilson, with their two children in this country, my cousin Mr. John Wilson, preacher at Medfield, and my cousin Mrs. Mary Davenport at Roxbury, one hundred and twenty pounds, that is, to each forty pounds apiece. And in case that either my cousin John or my cousin Davenport should die before they come to enjoy it, then their parts to be given to their children.

For the rest of my son's third part or what else should have accrued to him out of my estate by virtue of his executorship or my gifts, . . . I leave it to my overseers with the advice and consent of my wife while she remains alive to order and dispose of it to any such public or charitable use or uses to the town of Boston or to the College of Cambridge in New England or elsewhere that they or the greater part of them in their wisdom and consciences shall judge to be most useful and necessary, and in such a way that the main stock, be it more or less, if possible may still be preserved to the said uses and ends, as I have ordered in my other legacies of such kinds.

And my desire and request is to all my overseers that in case my son Benjamin should die before his daughter Hannah Keayne should be of age to enjoy her own estate, that they would be assistant to my wife, her grandmother, in their best counsel and advice, to dispose of her for her future education and learning unto some such wise and godly mistress or family where she may have her carnal disposition most of all subdued and reformed by strict discipline, and also that they would show the like care and assistance in seasonable time to provide some fit and godly match proportionable to her estate and condition that she may live comfortably and be fit to do good in her place and not to suffer her to be circumvented or to cast away herself for want of counsel and watchfulness upon some swaggering gentleman or others that will look more after the enjoying of what she hath than living in the fear of God and true love to her.

And my further desire and request to all my overseers is that if any, whether it be my executor, my wife, or any other, . . . having truly and justly received their own parts and legacies that I have in my will bequeathed to them, if they shall keep or desire to keep any further part of my estate in their hands or any of the legacies mentioned in this will [until] they come . . . due to be paid in (as some of them will be pretty long [at] first), that [my overseers] take good security from them for the several sums they shall so keep, or else to deliver them forth to such as will give security. [This I desire so] that what I have intended for good may not by miscarriage, want of discretion, or care to manage it well, or by any unfaithfulness come to sink or to be wasted and so the works to which they were given or any of the parties to whom the legacies do belong should be wholly or in part deceived or disappointed of that which out of my love for their good I have given to them, unless it plainly appear at the inventorying of my estate, or shortly after, that my estate will not reach to accomplish all things that I have given away in this will. [If this be the case] then my wife, my heir, and grandchild, with Anthony, Mary, and Benjamin Jupe, whom I am bound both in nature and grace first to take care of and they in conscience to receive and enjoy it, are to be first provided for out of my estate according to what I have given to them particularly. I say their legacies being paid or provided for, if any loss should be or any shortness of estate happen by the change of times or otherwise, it must be abated proportionably out of my other gifts to other persons and uses.

[*Kindness to Troublesome Kin*]

Item. I give and bequeath to the three children of my own sister Mrs. Grace Jupe now deceased, namely Anthony Jupe, Mary Jupe, now wife to John Morse of Boston, and Benjamin Jupe, now with me and under my care and tuition, one hundred pounds out of my own estate besides what is mentioned before out of my son's estate in case he should die, as above mentioned. Which hundred pounds I give after this manner: thirty pounds thereof unto my cousin Anthony Jupe to be paid to him or laid out for him in some such way as may bring him in something yearly, rather than to pay it to him at once [unless] he be in some settled way wherein it may appear to my executor and overseers that it will be more for his benefit and advantage to have it together than to have the benefit of it yearly. [In this case it is] to be paid to him or laid out for him within two years after my decease, if he be then living, and he [is to] pay to my executor or his assigns any such debt as shall appear then to be due to me from him at the time of my death, if any such debt should be.

Item. I give and bequeath unto my cousin Mary Jupe, now Mary Morse, thirty pounds more out of the above said hundred pounds to her own particular use and benefit, to be laid out within two years after my death in some such way that she may have the benefit of it coming in yearly for her supply, if she be then living. [But] if her husband should owe me anything at the time of my death that I have lent him or laid out for him or them before, I would have that deducted out of this thirty pounds. And if it should be above thirty pounds, then this legacy [is] to cease and to be accounted paid in the lieu of so much debt.

Item. I give and bequeath unto my cousin Benjamin Jupe (because he is lame and dim-sighted and not like to do much if anything at all towards his own maintenance) I give to him forty pounds, if he be living two years after my death. [This is to be] laid out in some such way or upon some such thing as may bring in a yearly profit towards his diet and clothing while he lives. At his death the stock itself [is] to be returned to my executor's heirs or assigns. This is besides the hundred pounds that I have given him before out of my son's estate in case he should die before he comes here. . . . If it please God he should marry to an honest careful woman with the advice and counsel of my wife and son Benjamin Keayne or by the advice and assistance of my overseers and he should have one child or more by her, then my will is that not only the profit of this forty pounds after the death of the father may be continued to the children or child of his, but that the stock itself may be divided between them.

And though Anthony Jupe [has] become to age and so fit to dispose of himself, and Mary Jupe is disposed of in marriage, and [they] have their means in their own hands (with which two I have reckoned and have set their accounts even, both of what I received by virtue of my executorship to their mother's will and what I laid out for them and upon them while they were under my tuition and care, and have full releases and discharges from them under both their hands in my white box in my closet at Boston upon which my cabinet stands) notwithstanding though they be now [away] from me and at their own disposing, all saving Benjamin, and notwithstanding all the care and pains that I took for them while they came to age, I would yet show the affection of an uncle towards them in desiring and seeking their good. And because I have no other nearer kindred in this country that I know of, nor none that I can so well confide in, or that I may make so bold with as my loving wife (and as I do heartily thank her for that care, pains, and love that she hath already showed to these three fatherless and motherless children since they came to me for my sake, they being otherwise untoward enough as children, without discretion and consideration, which I have kindly taken at her hands and do gratefully accept) my desire and request to her is that while she and they live in these parts that she would look after them and remember that they are the near kindred of a husband that hath truly and tenderly loved her, to own them and do for them by her continuous counsel, loving carriage towards them, and entertaining of them as need shall be. When they come to visit her or take advice of her about anything that is meet [she is] to suffer them to want nothing that she, without prejudice to herself, may help them unto (whilst they take good courses fit to be owned and carry themselves lovingly and respectfully towards her) and [that] their necessities and straits calls for, if any such thing may befall either of them. And the same request I make to my son Benjamin Keayne, to be assistant both to his mother and them, to do unto them all what good he can.

But if all or either of them shall grow proud, stubborn, undutiful, or troublesome either to my wife or son, or should go about to molest or vex either of them by the sinister instigation of themselves or others for them upon no just grounds, or shall cast out contemptuous or disgraceful speeches against them or myself after my death, of which I know no just cause, having as I said before reckoned with Anthony and Mary Jupe and examined all the accounts between us before witness and with the help of others chosen thereto and have their discharge and release (only with Benjamin I could not reckon, because he is not of years, but his accounts both of what I have received of his and laid out for him ever since he came to me is by itself in my vellum debt book and I would have all just right done unto him when his account comes to be examined and ended)—but if, [I say,] they should go about needlessly to molest or vex either my wife or son in any troublesome or reproachful way instead of thankfulness for all my love and care for so many years to them, then my will is that the legacies that I have given to . . . those that shall so carry themselves shall cease and be utterly void . . . and not be paid nor continued to them.

But for my cousin Benjamin Jupe because of his many infirmities and his inability otherwise to help himself I do in a special manner commend the care of him to the love and tenderness of my wife and son whom I have found to be very indulgent towards him and to see that he may not be wronged. He hath comfortable maintenance left him to bear the charge of his diet, apparel, and physic by four pounds a year left him by his mother in a house at London, also by some tenements in London left him by his uncle, Mr. Nicholas Jupe, which will produce 8 or ten pounds per anno to him for 18 or 20 years, besides what I have left him in this will. And [my desire is] if it should be thought convenient that he should marry for his future comfort and he [be] inclined to it, that then my wife and son would afford him the best advice and counsel in making choice of such a match for him as may be for his future comfort. And although possibly when he comes to age, myself being dead, he may desire to live with his sister Morse, which in some respects I should not dislike, yet if my wife be willing and find it convenient to keep him with her, I knowing her former care and tenderness to him, her skillfulness in sickness and health to provide for him, I think he can be nowhere better than with her. But if she should put him out to board from herself, then I think his own sister, Mrs. Morse, may be fitter to have him than a stranger, [unless] my son should keep a family here and would keep him in his own house in case his mother should refuse it. . . . Considering that my wife hath already undergone the trouble of his education from his childhood to this time, when he was far more sickly and troubled with such infirmities that few would have been willing to have received him into their house, not having means enough by half except for what he had from ourselves to defray the charges that must necessarily be laid out upon him, I do think it most fit that she before any other should have the keeping of him now when he is more out of trouble and [has] means to maintain himself, which he had not before. It were an ill requital of her former love and pains to take him from her now when there is less trouble in keeping him, if she be still willing to keep him. Possibly I should have done somewhat more for them at my death, but God has provided for them . . . comfortably by the death of another uncle in London who hath given to each of them 8 or 10 lb. a year apiece for 18 or 20 years and I have otherwise been at charge with them and have had many occasions of exercising my love towards them for so many years together since they have been with me. I think they have comfortable maintenance, if they be wise to improve it the best way for their own good.

[*Several Gifts to Friends and Relatives*]

Item. I give and bequeath to my loving brother Mr. John Wilson, our pastor at Boston, as a token of my love and thankfulness for all his kindness showed to me ten pounds, wishing that my estate were such that I could have done for him and his as I desire.

Item. I give and bequeath unto my loving sister his wife, my wife's own sister, ten pounds to be wholly at her own disposing and for her own particular use. Both these are to be paid to them within two years after my decease.

Item. I give and bequeath to my cousin Mr. John Wilson, my brother's son, now preacher at Medfield, thirty pounds. And in case he should die before he comes to receive this legacy, then I give twenty pounds of the said legacy to his child or children, to be equally divided between them in case he hath any alive at that time two years after my death.

Item. I give and bequeath twenty pounds to my cousin Mary, Wilson's sister, now Mrs. Davenport at Roxbury, if she be living two years after my decease.

Item. I give and bequeath unto Mrs. Cotton, the wife of our dear and reverend teacher, Mr. John Cotton, deceased, three pounds as a testimony of my respects unto her dear husband, in case she be alive and remain a widow within two years after my decease.

Item. I give and bequeath unto our elder Oliver, if he shall be alive one year after my decease, forty shillings as a token of my respects to him. And in case he should be dead before then, I bequeath the said legacy to his grandchild, the son of Mr. John Oliver, deceased, to be paid in for his use within two years after my decease, if he be then alive.

Item. I give and bequeath to our elder Colborne and our elder Penn thirty shillings apiece as a token of my love to them, to be paid within two years after my decease, if they be then alive.

Item. I give and bequeath unto Major General Gibbons as an acknowledgment of my thankfulness for his constant love to me, three pounds to buy him a ring or a piece of plate, to be paid two years after my decease, if he be then alive and dwelling in this country.

Item. I give and bequeath unto my ancient friend, Reverend Mr. Norton, three pounds in case his abode be with us here in Boston two years after my decease.

Item. I give unto our brother Reynolds, senior, shoemaker, twenty shillings as a token of my respects to him, if he be living two years after my decease, not forgetting a word that he spoke publicly and seasonably in the time of my distress and other men's vehement opposition against me.

Item. I give and bequeath unto Sarah Baker, the daughter of John Baker that was sometime my bail, and the child born in my house, forty shillings as a testimony of my respect to him, to be paid to her mother for the child's use, forty shillings in a heifer calf that shall be worth so much two years after my decease. If the child be then living [it is] to be kept and improved for her till she be married or comes of age to receive it herself. Some engagement is to be taken of the mother or her husband or who else it shall be committed to, that it shall be so kept for the child's use with all the increase of it, necessary charges for wintering, etc. being deducted for keeping.

Item. I give and bequeath to Edward Hall of Lynn, carpenter, as an acknowledgment of all his former faithfulness and loving service to me (though of later years he hath carried it less deserving and fuller oft more just provocation) three pounds, to be paid unto him two years after my decease, if he be then alive and owe me nothing. If he do, then to abate him so much of his just debt. If he should be dead and owe me nothing, then my will is that this three pounds may be improved to the use of his children till they come of age, and that security may be taken of those it is delivered to, that it shall be so disposed of.

Item. I give and bequeath to William Feavor, sometime my servant, forty shillings, and to Alice his wife who was also my servant, twenty shillings, if they be living two years after my decease. And if they should owe me anything, then deduct it out of their debt as I do to Edward Hall.

Item. I give and bequeath to Robert Rand of Lynn, sometime my servant, forty shillings, to be paid him within two years after my decease, if he be then living and in this country.

Item. I give and bequeath unto James Pemberton and his wife, sometimes my servant and now partner with me at my farm, forty shillings two years after my decease, if he be then living, desiring him if he be then at my farm that he would do the best he can in taking care of what I shall leave in his hands, and to be assistant to my wife and son in the best he can do for their good and benefit whilst he shall there remain, either in his care or best advice to them in disposing of the farm for their best advantage if he stay not in it himself at my son's request.

Item. I give and bequeath to my three negroes if they be living with me at the time of my death, namely to Angola, negro, forty shillings, and to Richard, my negro, forty shillings, and to his wife, Grace, negro, twenty shillings, to be paid to them in some young heifers to raise a stock for them two years after my decease. Yea, though they should be disposed of to any other place before by my executors and if they should be still kept or employed at my farm or in the service of my son or wife I hope they will be as diligent and careful in their business and as serviceable to them as they have been to me while I lived.

Item. I give the negro Richard's legacy to his daughter Zipora if she be alive at my death.

Item. I give and bequeath to Mr. Whiting, one of the teaching elders at Lynn, forty shillings to be paid two years after my decease, if he be then living and in this country.

Item. I give and bequeath to Mr. Cobbett, the other teaching elder at Lynn, forty shillings upon the same terms as Mr. Whiting hath his.

[A Miserable Ingrate Excluded]

Item. I give and bequeath to the two children of my wife's brother, Mr. John Mansfield, ten pounds, to be equally divided between them and to be paid in two cows to be kept for the use of the children, and the yearly profits of them to be allowed towards the children's maintenance yearly. But neither the cows nor the profits of them [are] to come into the hands of the father or mother, but [are] to be laid out upon the children either for clothes or diet. They that keep the cows [are] to give security to my executor or overseers, that they shall be so reserved for the children till they come to age. And if one of them should die, then the survivor [is] to enjoy that part with his own. If they should both die before they come to age, then . . . the cows and the benefit of them [are] to be to the use of the father, if he be then alive; if dead, then they are to return to my executor.

And if any should be inquisitive why I do no more for him or his, being a brother, my answer is that this which I have done is more with respect to his sister, my loving wife, than in reference to him who hath proved an unworthy and unthankful brother to me, though I have done very much for him in England divers times, in releasing him out of prisons, in paying his debts for him, in furnishing him with a stock to set up his trade when he had spent all his own, in taking up many quarrelsome businesses of dangerous consequence which he in his distempered fits had plunged himself into. Yet I compounded them for him, and at his sister's, my wife's, entreaty with some other friends of hers I sent him over into New England when his life was in some hazard. I paid his passage and some of his debts for him in England and lent him money to furnish himself with clothes and other necessaries for his voyage. For many years I found him diet and clothes gratis, till for his distempered carriages and unworthy behavior I was fain to put him out of my house, all the work that ever he did for me not being worth his clothes. Yet was he never quiet from disturbing my whole family and pursuing me with continual complaints to our elders and others, seeking to pull a maintenance out of my estate whilst himself lived idly and spent what he got in drink and company-keeping. So spiteful and envious was he to me, notwithstanding all my former care over him in seeking and endeavoring his good, that he would have cut my throat with his false accusations if it had lain in his power, as it well appeared when time was. Besides, he owes me between 20 and 30 lb. if not more (for 16 or 20 lb. of which I have his bond) for while he was in England, besides all that I have done for him since. Yet he denied this to be his hand before Mr. Winthrop, our then governor, and our elders, till he was plainly convinced and sharply reproved for his falseness. The rest [of the debt] is for what he hath had of me here, though nothing be put to account for his several years' diet, clothes, and other things while he lived in my house. Yet all this hath not been worth a good word, if his humor be not continually satisfied.

All my kindness hath been put into a broken bag and cast upon an unthankful person that hath ever rewarded my good with evil, though I desire to forgive him and pray to God also that He would forgive him all his false reports and sinful plots that he hath practised against me, when time was, for all the mercy and kindness that I have showed to him in his straits and necessities. And though some may think that these things had been better concealed and buried, yet seeing God hath not helped him to acknowledge his sin, nor truly to repent of it, in my apprehension in these respects I think it is of use to convince such [men] of their evil carriages and help them the more to take heed of the future when they see and feel what they lose by it, and not to think they have the liberty of their tongues to abuse their friends at their pleasure and yet look to have as great supplies from their friends and their estates as those that carry it more respectfully towards them. I think such vices are to be corrected this way when by other means they cannot be restrained. But his carriages in this kind are pretty well known to others now as they are to me, though at first they were not so ready to believe them but rather the contrary. Besides, I know I shall leave to my loving wife, his sister, a comfortable estate who I doubt not will be willing and ready to do somewhat for him if his carriage to her as it hath been to myself do not hinder it. They that do expect love from their friends had not need abuse them but rather show love and respect to them. I have the rather made mention of these things to vindicate myself from the censures of others who else might have thought the hardlier of me for seeming to neglect him.

[*His Sufferings in New England:* *Unchristian, Uncharitable, and Unjust Slanders*]

It may be some on the other side may marvel (especially some who have been acquainted with some expressions or purposes of mine in former wills) that I should give away so much of my estate in private legacies and to private uses which might better have been spared and to give little or nothing to any public use for the general good of the country and commonwealth [except] what I have appropriated to our own town of Boston.

To answer this doubt or objection I must acknowledge that it hath been in my full purpose and resolution ever since God hath given me any comfortable estate to do good withal, not only before I came into New England but often since, to study and endeavor both in my life and at my death to do what I could do to help on any public, profitable, and general good here. ... My thoughts and intents have been about the castle for public defense, the college and schools for learning, the setting up of a bridewell or workhouse for prisoners, malefactors, and some sort of poor people, stubborn, idle, and undutiful youth, as children and servants, to have been kept at work in either for correction or to get their living, and some other things that I need not mention. In which things, though I could not have done so much as I desired, yet so much I should have done as might have proved an example and encouragement to others of greater estates and willing minds to have done more and to have helped to carry them on to more perfection. For I have held it a great degree of unthankfulness to God that when He hath bestowed many blessings and a large or comfortable outward estate upon a man that he should leave all to his wife and children to advance them only by making them great and rich in the world or to bestow it upon some friends or kindred that it may be hath no great need of it and to dispose none or very little of it to public charitable or good works such as may tend to His glory and the good of others in way of a thankful acknowledgment to Him for so great favors.

But the truth is that unkindness and ill requital of my former love, cost, and pains both in Old England and here which I have taken to promote the good of this place has been answered by divers here with unchristian, uncharitable, and unjust reproaches and slanders since I came hither, as if men had the liberty of their tongues to reproach any that were not beneficial to them. [These attacks came] together with that deep and sharp censure that was laid upon me in the country and carried on with so much bitterness and indignation of some, contrary both to law or any foregoing precedent if I mistake not, and, I am sure, contrary or beyond the quality and desert of the complaints that came against me, which indeed were rather shadows of offense, out of a desire of revenge made great by the aggravations of some to make them heinous and odious than that they were so indeed, and this not in my own judgments only (which may be looked at as partial) but in the judgments of hundreds that have expressed themselves, both then and especially since. Yet by some it was carried on with such violence and pretended zeal as if they had had some of the greatest sins in the world to censure. . . . Had it been in their power or could they have carried it they would not have corrected or reformed but utterly have ruined myself and all that I had, as if no punishment had been sufficient to expiate my offense [of] selling a good bridle for 2 s. that now worse are sold without offense for 3 s., 6 d. nails for 7 d., and 8 d. nails for 10 d. per hundred, which since and to this day are frequently sold by many for a great deal more. And so [it was] in all other things proportionably, as selling gold buttons for two shilling nine pence a dozen that cost above 2 in London and yet were never paid for by them that complained.

These were the great matters in which I had offended, when myself have often seen and heard offenses, complaints, and crimes of a high nature against God and men, such as filthy uncleanness, fornications, drunkenness, fearful oaths, quarreling, mutinies, sabbath breakings, thefts, forgeries, and such like, which hath passed with fines or censures so small or easy as hath not been worth the naming or regarding. These [things] I cannot think upon but with sad thoughts of inequality of such proceedings, which hath been the very cause of tying up my heart and hands from doing such general and public good acts as in my heart I both desired and intended.

... Some out of pride and prejudice may misinterpret what I speak and slight anything that either I would or could have done and possibly will say it is as good lost as found and undone as done, rather than ... think themselves beholden to any man for their gifts.

To which I would reply that those which are willing to do least themselves are most ready to slight and undervalue what is done by others. But let such know that if they grow proud and high-minded and scorn the kindness and endeavors of others that desire to do more good than themselves, God can and it may be will bring such high spirits into a lower frame and put them into such a condition that they may stand in need of the help of as mean and as much despised persons as myself before they die. In the meantime it is not good for any to slight the least kindness of their brethren; though they should have no particular benefit by it, so the country may fare the better. Neither is it good for them to grieve the spirits of their brethren nor to oppress those they despise nor willingly to quench or discourage them in any good they intend, for the time will come when I and they, the judges and judged, shall stand naked before one throne, where there will be no respect of persons, when all sentences and the causes of them will be called over again before a greater judge and a higher tribunal than man's can be, where the accused shall have his just plea as well as his accusers, and where the sighs of the oppressed and wronged will be heard and a righteous sentence shall pass not according to jealousies, suspicious reports, and the clamors of envious and prejudiced persons incensed and stirring up others to join therein, but as the true nature of the case stands, without prejudice or partiality. For all these are but leaden rules to walk by and often lead into errors and mistakes, making a mote in some men to be a mighty beam and another man's mountain ... to be looked at as a small molehill.

I know [that] the loud complaints of such persons before mentioned (though the most of them I had never dealt withal for a penny nor they with me) and others that had were drawn in against their own minds and intents that had no cause nor ground of dissatisfaction in themselves as themselves have acknowledged was the cause of that sharp and severe censure more than the true nature of the things complained of did deserve. This I must needs say if I should say no more, for I now speak the words of a man as if ready to die and leave the world, when there is no cause to daub with my own conscience to justify evil nor to extenuate my own faults, which will again be called to account, if not before washed away in the precious blood of Jesus Christ.

[*Unjust Cries of Oppression and Excessive Gains*]

I did submit to the censure, I paid the fine to the uttermost, which is not nor hath been done by many (nor so earnestly required as mine was) though for certain and not supposed offenses of far higher nature, which I can make good not by hearsay only but in my own knowledge, yea offenses of the same kind. [My own offense] was so greatly aggravated and with such indignation pursued by some, as if no censure could be too great or too severe, as if I had not been worthy to have lived upon the earth. [Such offenses] are not only now common almost in every shop and warehouse but even then and ever since with a higher measure of excess, yea even by some of them that were most zealous and had their hands and tongues deepest in my censure. [At that time] they were buyers, [but since then] they are turned sellers and peddling merchants themselves, so that they are become no offenses now nor worthy questioning nor taking notice of in others. Yet [they cried] oppression and excessive gains, [when] considering the time that they kept the goods bought in their hands before they could or would pay and the quality or rather the business of their pay for kind, yea contrary to their own promises, instead of gains there was apparent loss without any gains to the seller.

The oppression lay justly and truly on the buyer's hand rather than on the seller; but then the country was all buyers and few sellers, though it would not be seen on that side then. For if the lion will say the lamb is a fox, it must be so, the lamb must be content to leave it. But now the country hath got better experience in merchandise, and they have soundly paid for their experience since, so that it is now and was many years ago become a common proverb amongst most buyers that knew those times that my goods and prices were cheap pennyworths in comparison of what hath been taken since and especially [in comparison with] the prices of these times. Yet I have borne this patiently and without disturbance or troubling the Court with any petitions for remission or abatement of the fine, though I have been advised by many friends, yea and some of the same Court, so to do, as if they would be willing to embrace such an occasion to undo what was then done in a hurry and in displeasure, or at least would lessen or mitigate it in a great measure. But I have not been persuaded to it because the more innocently that I suffer, the more patiently have I borne it, leaving my cause therein to the Lord.

Yet I dare not subscribe to the justness of that time's proceeding against me, nor did my conscience to the best of my remembrance ever yet convince me that that censure was either equal or deserved by me. I speak not this to grieve any godly heart or to lay any misinterpretation or scandal upon the whole Court or all the magistrates in general whom I have ever thought myself bound to honor and esteem and submit to in lawful things. And I am not ignorant of the great debates that was in the Court about this business and that the pretended zeal of some of the chief sticklers who drew what parties they could to their opinion was opposed by a considerable number both of the magistrates and deputies, and that there was no proof to witness nor no ground in law nor example to carry it as they did, and that there was more said by much in open Court in my defense than I speak here for myself, and that not [out of] respect or relation that they had to me, but from their own consciences and judgments and looked at it as most severe, though it may be they would not have wholly acquitted me. Yea, I know that the censure itself in that kind and measure as it passed was against the desire and judgment of almost the greatest number of the chiefest and wisest of the magistrates and deputies in that Court. For the fine was cast but by one vote, as I have been credibly informed by that one party himself as well as others. Those that did yield to what was done did consent rather to prevent a greater inconvenience (the opposite party harkening to no moderation nor reasons alleged) than approving of the sentence.

And our honored governor Mr. John Winthrop, which is now with God, though as I heard at that time was rather against me than for me, yet not long before his death at a meeting at Capt. Tyng's house, whither all our elders and some others with myself was invited, he, in his discourse with our reverend teacher Mr. Cotton and my brother Wilson, myself with others sitting close by, he took occasion of his own accord to speak of the proceedings of the Court in this business as if he had been troubled or had had his mind exercised about it, [and to say] that it was needful and just to consider of that act again. And by his speech it seemed to me and others that he had a purpose of his own accord to have moved the General Court to recall that censure that had passed against me, which was approved of by those he spoke it to. I did not think meet to make any reply or to give him occasion of further discourse about it, because he had not [that] I heard made mention of my name, though all understood whom he meant. Therefore, about 3 weeks or a month after, I went home to him and desired to know what his meaning was in such expressions that he had with our elders at such a time, and then he more plainly told me his meaning. I am confident that he hath been much troubled in himself, that things had passed then as they did, and that if he had lived he would have used his utmost endeavor that my fine at least should have been restored back to me. And not only himself but also some others not only of the magistrates, but of the deputies, yea some of them that were then against me, have said that they think the Court ought in justice to do no less than to give me money again.

Therefore, I hope that what I have here writ out of the grief and trouble of my heart will be no offense to those whom I reverence in the Lord and intend to lay no blemish upon in the least kind, nor to no moderate or impartial man that was then either of the Court or out of it, for I intend not to give them just offense. If others shall and will misconstrue my true meaning, I must leave them to God, unto Whom I have and shall still commit my cause and cry to Him for right. And I have many testimonies in my spirit that He hath righted me therein, not only in the hearts and judgments of many men that knew and heard of those proceedings, but also in my very outward estate, that though some intended it for my great hurt, yet God hath been pleased to turn it to my good so that I have not since fared the worse nor lost by it but hath since carried me through many and great engagements with comfort.

And it is not unusual in wills for men in their last and dying testaments when they shall speak no more to make mention of such things as have troubled them in their lives and such acts as they could not submit to in their judgments which they have done in their sufferings. I could mention some in my own time that I know, besides others I have read on. I will only mention one, Mr. Humphrey Fenn, a famous minister at Coventry, well known to many in this country, a nonconformist and therefore silenced by the bishops. In his last will and testament he made a full and open protestation against prelacy and the ceremonies for which he had suffered. But the times being then very corrupt the prelatical party, when the will came to be proved, would not suffer that part of his will to be put upon the records of their court.

Seeing there is a liberty given to the members of this Court and to others out of the Court, that if any acts pass and they cannot concur with the general vote to make their remonstrance or protestation of dissent, [if] it be done modestly and without provoking expressions, I hope, therefore, it will not be offensive for myself, that have been and now am a member of the Court (when I first drew out this declaration in a former will) and also a member both of church and commonwealth (though unworthy) to relate the state of my case and declare my own judgment and dissent (yea the judgments of hundreds more besides myself) in a case which doth so nearly concern me and wherein I conceive I have received so much wrong by the practices of some that I forbear to name though I could point them out and have observed and could tell of God's dealings with some of them since. But I forbear.

Therefore, I would make this request to the overseers of this my will, that all or some of them would (if they in their wisdom judge it not very inconvenient) to take a seasonable time to move the General Court about it, to recall or repeal that sentence and to return my fine again after all this time of enjoying it, . . . which I believe is properly and justly due to my estate and will not be comfortable for the country to enjoy. I make no doubt but it will willingly be hearkened to, though myself for some reasons sought it not while I lived, though advised to it. I conceive it would be much for their honor and would justify them in the hearts of many so to do and would be no cause of grief to any of them in the great day of account, no not to them that were then most forward and zealous of the prosecution. . . . And were it possible for me to know it certainly before I die (though it be not for the love of the money nor for addition to my estate by it, though it was a considerable sum, about eighty pounds, as I remember) it would much ease and refresh my spirit in respect of the equity of it. And if upon this motion of my overseers the Court shall be pleased to consent, . . . my will is that what is so returned by them may be given to Harvard College at Cambridge, according as I have proposed in my former gifts to that place, or [to] any other work more needful upon which it may be disposed of to more good or public use or service. This I leave to the discretion of my overseers with the consent of my executors.

[He Is Innocent of the Heinous Sin of Usury: The Entire Truth of the Matter]

But some that shall read or hear of the expressions in this my will will be ready to say [that] if I am and have been of this mind so long, how can it stand with that humble confession that I made both in the Court and in the church, when I endeavored in the one and did in the other give satisfaction, without carrying a great appearance of hypocrisy or at least of repenting my repentings.

I desire in this to clear my conscience both towards God and man and do not think that these things are improper to be mentioned in a will but very natural and suitable to it. Therefore I say, first, if my confession was humble and penetential, as is objected, [then] it did justly call for mercy and clemency and not for advantage and more severity, as some made use of it to that end (but with what equity I leave both them and it to the Lord, to Whom they must give an answer if some of them have not already done it, and to such a time wherein they may stand in need of mercy themselves and shall not find it; for there shall be judgment merciless to them that show no mercy). If my confession was not humble and penitent then the objection is needless. But I am glad the prevailing party at that time so took it, though they look upon it as an act of my guilt and use it as a weapon against me. But I think it will be a witness against them for their perverting of it.

I did not then nor dare not now go about to justify all my actions. I know God is righteous and doth all upon just grounds, though men may mistake in their grounds and proceedings, counsel have erred and courts may err and a faction may be too hard and outvote the better or more discerning part. I know the errors of my life. The failings in my trade and otherwise have been many. Therefore from God [the censure] was most just. Though it had been much more severe I dare not so open my mouth against it, nor never did as I remember, [except to] justify Him. Yet I dare not say nor did I ever think (as far as I can call to mind) that the censure was just and righteous from men. Was the price of a bridle, not for taking but only asking, 2 s. for [what] cost here 20 d. such a heinous sin? [Such bridles] have since been commonly sold and still are for 2 s. 6 d. and 3 s. or more, though worse in kind. Was it such a heinous sin to sell 2 or 3 dozen of great gold buttons for 2 s. 10 d. per dozen that cost 2 s. 2 d. ready money in London, bought at the best hand, as I showed to many by my invoice (though I could not find it at the instant when the Court desired to see it) and since was confirmed by special testimony from London? The buttons [were not even] paid for when the complaint was made, nor I think not yet; neither did the complaint come from him that bought and owed them nor with his knowledge or consent, as he hath since affirmed, but merely from the spleen and envy of another, whom it did nothing concern. Was this so great an offense? Indeed, that it might be made so, some out of their ignorance would needs say they were copper and not worth 9 d. per dozen. But these were weak grounds to pass heavy censures upon.

Was the selling of 6 d. nails for 8 d. per lb. and 8 d. nails for 10 d. per lb. such a crying and oppressing sin? And as I remember it was above two years before he that bought them paid me for them (and not paid for if I forget not) when he made that quarreling exception and unrighteous complaint in the Court against me, (he then being of the Court himself) that I had altered and corrupted my book in adding more to the price than I had set down for them at first delivery. If I had set down 8 d. after 2 years' forbearance for what I would have sold for 7 d. if he had paid me presently, I think it had been a more honest act in me than it was in him that promised or at least pretended to pay me presently that he might get them at a lower price than a man could well live upon, and when he had got my goods into his hands to keep me 2 or 3 years without my money. All that while there was no fault found at the prices, but when he could for shame keep the money no longer, yet he will requite it with a censure in the Court. For my own part, as I did ever think it an ungodly act in him, so I do think in my conscience that it had been more just in the Court to have censured him than me for this thing, though this was the chiefest crime alleged and most powerfully carried against me. Other things, as some farthing skeins of thread, etc., were drawn in to make this the more probable and to help to make up a censure. But the truth of the thing was this:

This man sent unto me for 2 or three thousand of 6 d. nails. I sent to him a bag full of that sort just as they came to me from Mr. Foote's in London, never opened nor altered by me. These I entered into my book at 8 d. per lb. thinking he would have paid me in a very short time. It fell out that these nails proved somewhat too little for his work. He sent them [back] again and desired me to let him have bigger [ones] for them. I took them and sent him a bag of 8 d. nails of the same quantity at 10 d. per lb. Now because I was loath to alter my book and to make a new charge I only altered the figures in my book and made the figure of "6" a figure of "8" for 8 d. nails and the figure of "8" that before stood for 8 d. a lb. I made "10 d." Now though he knew of the change of these 6 d. nails for 8 d. (which I had quite forgot through my many other occasions and the length of time that they had stood in the book unpaid) yet this he concealed from me and from the Court also. To make the matter more odious he challenged me and my book of falsehood, supposing that because he had kept me so long from my money therefore by altering the figures I had made the price higher than at first I had charged them down, and that I required 10 d. per lb. for 6 d. nails. And so carried it in the Court (where he was the more easily believed because he was a magistrate and of esteem therein, though it was a most unjust and untrue charge, and only from his own imagination), till I cleared it by good testimony from an honest man in his own town whom he sent for the first nails and [who] brought them back and received the bigger nails for them. [This man] came to me of his own accord and told me he heard there was a difference between such a man and I, which he said he could clear, and related the matter fully to me which I was very glad to hear. [His words] brought all things to my mind, [especially] what was the ground of altering the figures in the book, which before I had forgot though I saw it was done with my own hand. And this was the very truth of the thing. I presently acquainted our honored governor Mr. John Winthrop and some others who were very glad that the truth of that reproach was so unexpectedly discovered and cleared. Many if not most of the Court was satisfied with it, and saw the thing to be very plain in my debt book. But the party himself would not be satisfied, [insisting that] they were 6 d. nails set down at 10 d. per lb., though [he] himself saw the figure of "8" as plain as the figure of "10."

Now I leave it to the world or to any impartial man or any that hath understanding in trade to judge whether this was a just offense or so crying a sin for which I had such cause to be so penitent (this being the chief [accusation] and pressed on with so great aggravation by my opposers) [or whether] my actions, innocent in themselves, were misconstrued. I knew not how to help myself, especially considering it was no oppressing price but usual with others at that time to sell the like so and since [then] frequently for almost half as much more, as I think all know, and yet both given and taken without exception, or at least without public complaint. Yea, the same gentleman himself, since he hath turned merchant and trader, seems to have lost his former tenderness of conscience that he had when he was a buyer and is not so scrupulous in his own gains.

. . . If I be not misinformed, and I think I had it from very good information of some of his neighbors yet living that knew well what they said, he agreed with some of the neighbors in his own town that he would send for or bring with him 1000 lb. worth of English goods for the good of the country, which they should have at easy rates, and [that] he would take wheat, peas, or any sort of corn and cattle for the pay. They provided their pay according to agreement, but he failed them in their first expectation, having no goods come at all. Yet another year he had a less quantity come, and amongst them nails (and I believe taken up upon credit and not paid for before they came). Yet when they were come, corn nor cattle would not serve for pay, nor trust he would not, but his demands are ready money, and for the gains he will have 6 d. in the shilling profit (which was oppression and exaction in the highest degree when he was a buyer). And that was not all neither, for if they paid in Spanish money they must pay him their dollars at 4 s. 6 d. apiece, which here went currently at 5 s. And for his nails, they being scarce at that time, his neighbors being in want would have given him any price or pay for them, but he would part with none of them—no necessity would prevail except they would buy all his other goods with them, which no doubt came at prices high enough. This made his parcel lie somewhat long upon his hands and possibly [he] was fain to [drop] both in his price and pay after so many had refused them, and to retail some of them. For I myself was showed some cloth bought of him at 18 or 20 s. per yard that if some others had sold the like at 15 s. per yard it would have been thought worthy [of] complaint.

And let me add one thing more of his practice. Having obtained his desire against me in the Court, though not so fully as he would have had it, but being disappointed of his expectation in the church, they not looking upon the complaints and witnesses as the Court did, he undertook another unjust and unworthy attempt against me. He not only demanded but earnestly pursued me for 200 lb. which he pretended I owed him. I told him I never owed him 5 shillings in my life. He said it was for 200 lb. that his father had lent me in London and had assigned him to receive it, which he never did. I told him I never borrowed any money of his father in my life, but at his request did receive some money, of which there was 200 lb. left which he desired me [to let] lie by till he sent for it. This I did accordingly and had paid it long before I came out of England. This was about 2 years before I came to New England, when this gentleman came often to my house and received many courtesies from me (though now they were all forgot), and in all that time he never mentioned any such thing to me (for he knew it was paid) nor in 2 years or thereabouts after we had been in New England, till this falling out.

Nothing that I could say would satisfy him. Many letters passed between him and I but nothing would do except I could prove the payment of it, which I was not able to do, it being so long ago and things much out of mind and many things passing through my hands in so great a removal from one country to another. Yet I thought I did not part with such a sum of money without taking a receipt for it. I looked [through] all my papers and writings where I thought it might be, but could find none. For in such a remove many writings might be lost, or at least so mixed with other things so long out of date that there might be no hope of finding it. This made him more confident, so that he threatened very seriously to sue me for it in the Court.

But first, that he might carry on his design the better and make me the more odious, he made a great complaint to our elders of my false dealing with him, because he thought they had been too favorable to me in the former business. He writ a very tart letter and full of complaints against me to our reverend teacher Mr. John Cotton and pastor my brother Wilson. They acquainted me with it. I desired to see his letter which they gave to me. Having read it I denied his accusations and related plainly to them all things that I remembered about it. They seemed to be satisfied with my answer. They returned him an answer and wished me to write to him also. But nothing would satisfy him, but he desires a hearing before all our elders. (And he being a magistrate it could not without some show of disrespect be denied to him.) They acquainted me with it and I consented. A time was appointed when he and I should meet before all our 4 elders. I perceived now that what he did was not only in passion, but [that he] very seriously intended to make me pay that 200 lb. twice over, he having got an advantage against me both from my words and in my writing, that I had once such a sum left with me by his father. I began now to look over all my writings more carefully to see if I could find any writings that might clear the matter or give any light to me about it.

At last by a singular providence of God I found a clear and full receipt in one of my books, to whom I had paid his 200 lb., where and by whose order. It did much refresh me that I should now be able to clear my own innocency and be able to discover the falseness and unjustness of his accusations. But I kept this private to myself that I might see how far he would carry it and the uttermost that he intended to do, knowing this would help me at a dead lift. At the time appointed we met before our 4 elders. He opened his complaints and made his accusations against me very plausible. They put him in mind that possibly he might forget and that he would consider better of it. No, he was sure of it, and professed before them that he never had a penny of it from me, nor any other for him by his order, nor never had any account from any man about it. He carried it as if I did go about to cozen and deceive him of it. And [then] I made the unlikeliness of such a thing [clear] and demanded if it were so why he in all that 2 years before I came to New England did not demand it of me, (he also knowing of my purpose to come) when things were fresh in memory and where I had opportunity many ways to clear it or else to have paid it again. He was so passionately zealous that he intended as certainly to have made me pay it again as I was certain that I had paid it once before. When [I had said] all that I could say and [when] our elders did say [as much] as they apprehended in so dark a business (wherein there was no evidence on either side [except] what I myself had acknowledged) [and I saw that] I could give him no satisfaction, then I desired them to give me some time to look amongst my writings again for the receipt. This was granted me and another time of meeting set.

When we came [together again] I kept my book closed and desired to know whether in that time he had not called to remembrance something about the payment of it, or whether he was not indebted to some man that he might have appointed to receive it for him (for by the receipt I perceived that his father had either given or lent him this 200 lb.). [When he] still utterly denied this I then produced my receipt for it. He read it and they all perused it and saw it fair writ by him that received the money. He acknowledged that he knew the gentleman, a linen draper in Cornhill, and that he had dealings with him then and when he came for New England. But [he] still said he had no account of him for this 200 lb. I told him that could not be, but if he had not, it did not concern me. I charged him before them of the great injury that he had and farther would have done to me if the Lord had not cleared my innocency by the finding of this receipt. And I told them that I would write myself to the linen draper about it; and though he could not excuse it yet he had not a heart to submit so low as to acknowledge any fault to me.

When he was gone I told our elders that [I] intended to sue him for the slanders and injury that he had done to me. Mr. Cotton wished me rather to forbear because of my late troubles and that it was no time for recriminations, but [that] after things were a little blown over, it might be more seasonable to do it. I followed his counsel, yet said I should not only clear my own innocency by it but also set him out in his colors both in this and his former prosecutions of me.

But it may be some will allege in his defense that this was but his forgetfulness, it being so long ago, and that doubtless he would not purposely have wronged me in so great a sum as that was.

The greater the sum was, the greater was his temptation to do it. If his forgetfulness should excuse him in telling so many untruths and affirming positively so many false things why should not my forgetfulness have excused [my knowing] not where my receipt was? And why when I spake the truth that I had paid the money, though I did not certainly know when nor to whom, with some other circumstances forgot, [was this] rejected and all that I could say esteemed of no value to him?

I must needs say that I cannot readily be of their belief that so think, though possibly there might be a slight, or a kind of willing forgetfulness. But I appeal to all that know the man and knew his estate both then and since as well as I did, whether it be a thing likely that such a lump as 200 lb. should sink down and be so drowned in his estate that he could not miss it in 3 or 4 years together, [especially] when things were more fresh in his memory; or that he should appoint another to receive it of me and yet himself neither owed it to that man before nor received nothing of him for it since; or [that I] was not by either of them brought to account, neither before he came to New England (when in all likelihood they would reckon having had dealings together) nor never since. I know in those days he stood in as much money as other of his neighbors and that the removing from one country into another for habitation is very chargeable and puts many of good estates to some straits for want of money to even and discharge many expenses and debts. Therefore, that he should let 200 lb. lie in my hands so many years without receiving any profit or forbearance for it, yea and quite forget to call for it or to require some note under my hand or some security that he might have had something to show him that I did owe him so much, seeing he was to leave the land and go on so long and dangerous a voyage by sea, it is to me so incredible that I cannot believe it.

But this I do believe, that if I had dealt so by him and affirmed so resolutely things that were false and untrue, though it had been for the getting of a far less sum than 200 lb. from him, he would not only have judged me to be a liar and a very false and deceitful man, but would have made the world believe that I would have cozened him of so much money and would have thought me worthy to have stood in the pillory or to have suffered some other severe punishment that might have made me an example to all others. [So] it well appeared by his violent prosecutions of me in the Court for far smaller offenses than this, his nails having the greatest show. Yet if some could have had their wills they would have had the fine mounted up to 1000 lb., yea 500 lb. was too little except some corporal punishment was added to it, such as my man's standing openly on a market day with a bridle in his mouth, or at least about his neck, as I was credibly informed. Here was well guided zeal.

. . . I was much grieved and astonished to be complained of in Court and brought publicly to answer as a grievous malefactor only upon the displeasure of some that stirred in it more than properly did concern them and to be prosecuted so violently for such things as seemed to myself and others so trivial, and upon great outcries, as if the oppression had been unparalleled. And when all things were searched to the bottom nothing of moment was proved against me worthy of mention in a court but what I have here expressed. Yet no other way [was] left me for help, things being carried so highly against me by one party, as I had it by good informations, but by casting myself upon the favor or mercy of the court, as some had counseled me. Since, though, I think they have had cause to be grieved for as well as I because it had an effect contrary to expectation. The means which should have procured the more clemency was by some made an argument of my greater guilt. If this should convince me of the equity and honesty of such men's moderation who delight to turn things not to the best but worst sense, the Lord help me to see that which yet I have not done. This was not the way to bow and melt my heart, but rather to provoke it to cry more earnestly to God to do me right in such a case.

I confess still as I did then and as I have said before, that the newness and strangeness of the thing, to be brought forth into an open court as a public malefactor, was both a shame and an amazement to me. It was the grief of my soul (and I desire it may ever so be in a greater measure) that any act of mine (though not justly but by misconstruction) should be an occasion of scandal to the Gospel and profession of the Lord Jesus, or that myself should be looked at as one that had brought any just dishonor to God (which I have endeavored long and according to my weak ability desired to prevent), though God hath been pleased for causes best known to Himself to deny me such a blessing. And if it had been in my own power I should rather have chosen to have perished in my cradle than to have lived to such a time. But the good pleasure of God is to keep me low in my own eyes as well as in the eyes of others, and also to make me humble and penitent, lest such mercies should have lifted me up above what is meet. Yet I do say still as I have often done before, that those things for which I was questioned (in the best apprehension, guided by God's word, that I had then or have since attained to) did deserve no such proceedings as was carved out to me, though some blew up those sparks into a great flame. And I am not alone herein, though it was my own case, but many wise and godly servants of the Lord, as well as divers others were and still are of the same mind. Yea, some that were then much against me have confessed since to me that things were carried in a hurry.

[Action of the Church After an Exquisite Search]

Yea, and our own church, when they called all those complaints over again that was laid to my charge (as it was meet they should) to see how far there was equity in them and how far I was guilty of all those clamors and rumors that then I lay under, they heard my defense equally and patiently, and after all their exquisite search into them and attention to what others could allege or prove against me, they found no cause but only to give me an admonition. Less they could not do without some offense, considering what had passed in Court before against me. Now if the church had seen or apprehended or could have proved that I had been so justly guilty as others imagined, they could have done no less than to have excommunicated and cast me out of their society and fellowship as an unworthy member.

But it may be some will reply to this that [though] my offenses might be looked at with the same eye in the church as it was in the court my penitency and godly or at least seeming sorrow might keep off the church's censure though it would not the Court's.

It is true that in anything wherein I might justly take shame or sorrow to myself God inclined my heart not to withstand it, for he that hides his sins shall not prosper, but he that confesseth and forsaketh them shall find mercy. In many [ways] we all sin in this. And who can say his heart is clean? Yet for the chief of the things that was most urged against me in Court and for which the sentence was passed against me, as the gold buttons, the bridle, the nails, the falsifying of my book, I did justify and stand to maintain that they was evident mistakes and that I was wronged about them: that they were 8 d. nails at 10 d. per lb. and not 6 d., that the buttons were gold and not copper, and that they cost 2 s. 2 d. per dozen in London, sold here at 2 s. 10 d. per dozen, and that there was no oppression in that price, that though the figures in my book were altered, yet it was not for any such end as was pretended and urged against me, but upon that very cause that before I have related. Here I had no cause of penitency or confession of guilt [unless] it was for having been so used and reproached about them against all equity. But if they should have cast me out of the church 20 times for this I should have chosen it rather than to have confessed myself guilty for [anyone's] satisfaction wherein I knew myself (better than any else did) to be innocent. . . . There was at the same time many in the church at this examination who was of the Court and had their vote in my censure, that heard what my speeches were both in the Court and in the church, and if there had been any contradiction, falsehood, or contrary recantation in them I should have heard of it to my farther prejudice. Yet I was more open and free in the church in clearing the thing for which I had suffered those troubles than I was in the Court.

[*This Christian Apologia Defended*]

I have been the longer and more particular in this relation to ease my own oppressed spirit which hath not been a little burdened about this thing and to leave a testimony of my innocency, so far as I was innocent, to the world behind me and [to show] how apprehensive I was and still am of the injury I then received therein. Neither have I related nor left this testimony behind me to censure or cast a reproach upon the whole Court, either upon all the magistrates or all the deputies, for I am not ignorant how and by whom this was acted and carried on principally and how many in the Court (both in their judgment and arguing with strong reasons against the illegality of their proceedings) would have freed and acquitted me. I lay the blame only upon such whose self ends and private prejudice did chiefly act them in this work. I speak this of and to brethren who I know do not look at all their acts and proceedings [as] so perfect but that mistakes and misapprehensions may break in and prevail sometimes and yet may be carried on like a mighty river that no banks can stay nor keep . . . within bounds. And therefore I hope none will be offended but will attend at any time to reason and to the just defense that any grieved or wronged brother shall make (seeing what was my case then may prove any of theirs another time), when it is proposed in meekness of spirit, for the clearing of themselves and their own innocency and easing of the heaving burdens of their hearts, as I have done at this time and with as much moderation as I can. For I know it is not lawful to speak evil of dignities nor to revile the rulers of the people nor to curse them in our hearts though they should be evil or do evil to us, but labor to leave it patiently and to commend all to God that judgeth righteously. This I have endeavored to do. [For] I know that [since] pagans and tyrants sometimes have admitted and mildly received and well interpreted and taken in good part the just apologies that some who have been oppressed by them have writ in their own defense, then those that are godly and Christian will do it much more. Therefore, I hope none will misconstrue my true meaning in this my will, nor draw my expression by any aggravations contrary to what I have intended herein. And for myself I desire patiently to bear the indignation of the Lord, because I have sinned against Him.

But it may be some will object that the whole Court joined together in my censure, and therefore I could not be looked at as innocent in the judgment of any of them.

I cannot safely say that they all joined in my censure, for some might be and I think were neuters and so did not vote at all in it. Neither do I say that I was so innocent that I deserve no reproof. But this I do say, that many in the Court stood to free me and endeavored so to do, but when that came to vote they had not number enough to carry it. [When] the question was what my fine should be, some flew high and named 1000 lb.; others mentioned 500 lb.; some again would have had it but 30 lb. or a less sum; others came to 80 lb. So when those that would have cleared me quite could not carry it for the least sum mentioned, yet they carried it against the greater sums. When it came to vote again they carried it from the 500 lb. proposers to those that had proposed 80 lb., and that was not because they thought the complaint deserved so great a fine. They did it to prevent the greater fine, for had not those that would have freed me concurred with them that voted for 80 lb. then the other party had carried it for 500 lb.

It may be some may demand how this can stand with a good conscience that I should keep in memory such unkindnesses as I have mentioned in this will so long (and some of these prejudices are against brethren and others) to my dying day, and whether these things had not better been quite buried and concealed. How could I with any comfort receive that blessed sacrament of love and keep communion with such either publicly or privately of whose carriages and actions I have such hard thoughts, and how it will stand with that rule of God's word which commands us to love the brethren, to do good to them that hate us, to pray for them that persecute us, or forgive our enemies, and to overcome the evil with our goodness?

I answer the rather because I desire to clear myself from such offenses and to satisfy such scruples as lie in my way and to give a reason for all my proceedings in these particulars, that I may do things in faith and not out of a passionate and discontented spirit and that to satisfaction if it may be. For I desire to walk according to the rule of a good conscience in all things and not knowingly to allow myself in any evil way. And if herein I should err it is for want of light and not against it. Therefore, I say there is many good and profitable uses to be made by remembering such actions of unkindness and other providences of God that have befallen us in our lives, though friends or brethren have been chief instruments therein, and how God hath delivered us or stood by us in such trials and afterwards, so [long as] this remembrance be not in malice and wrong in our hearts.

There may be just occasions not only to remember but to speak of them also, though I do or have forgiven them. Our Saviour remembers His disciples' unkind forsaking of Him and flying from Him in so great a time of need, and Peter's unthankful denying and forswearing of them. And He not only speaks of it but puts it upon record for all generations to take notice of. And yet He loved them, forgave them, and kept communion with them; and so doth the apostle Paul often. Our Saviour Christ, who hath left Himself [as] an example, keeps in memory and records the unkind usage of many cities and towns and the injuries that He received of His unthankful countrymen to His dying day. So the prophets and apostles not only remember but speaks how they carried it both in their courts and counsels against them. The scriptures are full of example. My brethren, the sons of my mother, have smitten me, yet that did not hinder them from a loving converse or private communion with them and a readiness to do them good as opportunity was offered. Much less might such unkindnesses hinder their own acceptable partaking of the Lord's Supper, though they did, as it were, tie the hands of our Saviour and His disciples or restrain them from doing so much good in those places and to such persons as otherwise they would have done. Joseph forgets not the unkindness of his brethren to his death and speaks of it then and that without sin for ought I perceive by the scriptures. Jacob in his last will and testament remembers and records the offenses of his children and the injuries of some of them against himself. He blesseth some and sharply reproves others and seems to be much prejudiced against their actions and practice though they were public persons rather than private. And yet he loves them, kept communion with them, and no doubt had forgiven them.

Unkindness and injurious offenses may be mentioned, though a man hath in his own heart either passed them by or quite forgiven them, [in order] to bring them to a sight of such evils by which they have so offended and grieved another which before they might not so well have considered or had before more slightly passed over with less consideration; and that they may have occasion to call over such actions again that they had forgot; and that so if they find evil in them they may now have the better opportunity to repent of them and to give satisfaction to those they have offended or wronged and to be the more watchful that they may not deal so with others. Yea it is a question whether a Christian be bound or that God requires it at their hands fully to forgive and finally forget all sinful unkindnesses or injuries till the parties that have done the wrong do see their sin and say it repents them and seek reconciliation and forgiveness of them. So it was with Joseph to his brethren, and so our savior Christ saith if our brother say it repents him, then thou shall forgive him often. It is true if my enemy were in great extremity and I knew it and could help him I were bound to do it and to do good for their evil, yea, to them that hate me, as I desire to do. Yet their unkindness may justly deprive them of a greater measure of bounty that might be intended towards them than what is given to them for their necessity. And though I should overcome evil with good, yet all a man's charity is not to be limited to them when there be divers others that stand in as much need that have never given such offenses and may be fitter objects of such fruits of love, who will be more thankful to God and them for it. Yea I think it is fit that they should see they lose somewhat and fare the worse for such carriages and misbehaviors towards those whom they should have showed more respect and love unto. And this much for satisfaction to all objections.

[Disposal of Property Resumed: His Wife's Third]

Now concerning my wife's third which I have given her to enjoy for her comfort and benefit during her natural life out of my houses, lands, and tenements—when it shall please God to take her out of this frail and temporal life, I do dispose of the same in manner and form following.

Item. I give and bequeath the one-half part thereof unto my son and heir, Major Benjamin Keayne, to his own proper use if he be then alive at his mother's death. And the other half part of this third which my wife enjoyed in her lifetime I divide into two equal parts, the one of which parts, or the full value thereof, I give and bequeath to my son's daughter and my grandchild, Hannah Keayne.

Item. I give and bequeath the other half part of this third or the due value thereof (in case my executor should desire to keep the land or housing to himself) unto Harvard College at Cambridge in New England, to be employed in the best way for the encouragement of learning, either for the better help and relief of the poorer and godlier sort of scholars or towards fellowships, as I have proposed in my forgoing gifts mentioned, to that place and use according to the best advice and counsel of the President and Overseers or Feoffees of that College that now are or then shall be, they taking in the advice and consent of my executor and overseers of this my will that now are or that then shall be living.

And if it shall please God that my son Benjamin Keayne should die before his mother, if he have any other children lawfully begotten of his body besides Hannah Keayne then my will is that those children shall enjoy and possess as their own all my right, title, and interest in and to that half part of my wife's third which before I had bequeathed to himself in case he had lived. [This is] to be equally divided between them and to be improved to their best benefit and advantage till they come of age to receive it into their own hands. If he have but one child more than Hannah, then that one child is to have it all. But if he should have no other child but Hannah Keayne then I give and bequeath that half part of my son's given to him out of my wife's third unto the use and benefit of the library in Boston, if it be set up and carried on as I have before mentioned in this will. I mean to buy fit books for the increase of that library. But if it be not built and carried on as I have before proposed, then I give this legacy or half part unto the use and benefit of the College of Cambridge to be improved for the best benefit thereof as I have expressed in my before mentioned legacies to the said place.

[An Unnatural Daughter-in-Law Excluded]

My mind and will further is that whatsoever I have given in this my will to my grandchild Hannah Keayne as her legacy and portion, whether it be the first three hundred pounds or any other gift that may befall her out of my estate by virtue of this my will, may be so ordered and disposed that her unworthy mother (sometimes the unnatural and unhappy wife of my son, that proud and disobedient daughter-in-law to myself and wife) Mrs. Sarah Dudley, now Sarah Pacy, may have no part nor benefit in or by what I have thus bestowed upon her daughter. For it is not my will but directly against it that she who hath walked so unworthily (that I may give it no worse terms) to us all should have any relief or anything to maintain her in her pride and contempt from anything that ever was accounted mine. Not that I would encourage the child to any rebellion, stubborn or undutiful carriage towards her mother. For God may break her heart and give her true and unfeigned repentance for all her former evil carriages and so [she] may justly deserve pity and compassion, if she should stand in need. If God should cast any other estate upon her by her father or grandmother, by a husband or otherwise, and if the child's love and duty or the mother's necessity and want should call for any such help or assistance from her, I shall not restrain her, but leave her to her own liberty that way. But for any estate that I have given to Hannah Keayne (I yet seeing no change or unfeigned repentance in her mother) I do here charge and require my son, her father, and do earnestly and heartily desire all my overseers that they would take care to see as others so this part of my will fulfilled, that her mother may have nothing to do nor have any benefit by any part of my estate that I have given for the comfort and support of her daughter.

If her mother should go about or so far prevail with her daughter by her insinuations or the daughter out of natural pity or respect to her mother should be acting that way or that she should seek to draw her in to be engaged for her before these legacies comes to her hands upon hope of receiving these or paying anything out of them when they shall grow due, and that Hannah refuse to hearken to the counsel of her father and my overseers herein but follows her own or mother's mind herein or those that shall advise her that way contrary to this which I have declared to be my will—then my will is that all my legacies from first to last given and intended by me to Hannah Keayne in that case do cease and become utterly void to any use or purpose as concerning her, saving what of it shall be disbursed and laid out of it about her maintenance and education during the time of her minority till she was capable by virtue of this my will to have received it into her own hands. And what I have before so given to her, I do now give, if the same in the cases before mentioned, to her father, my son Benjamin Keayne, and if he should be then dead, then to his other child, or if he have more than one, to them equally between them. And in case he should have no other children but she, then I give it to the College at Cambridge in New England for the best furthering of learning there, as I have ordered in former gifts to them, if she prove obstinate therein.

And my will concerning Hannah Keayne further is that she have no relation to her mother in respect of her education and training up or any abode with her, or putting her out to board or learning, but my desire is that her father and grandmother may have the care of her education and may either keep her themselves or rather put her forth to some such place where with the best care she may be trained up in the fear of God and her spirit subdued and kept in from outward extravagances, and [that] the profit or benefit of her legacies be improved to discharge the cost of her learning, apparel, and diet, [unless] her father and grandmother will be at that charge as I have hitherto been, and then to let the improvement of her legacy or legacies be kept for an increase of her portion and added thereto. And in case her grandmother should die before she comes to years fit to receive her portion and her father should either be absent out of this country or dead, my desire is that my brother and sister Wilson would take the care and charge of her protection and education with themselves or else to find out some fit place with the advice of my overseers to which she may be commended, and that they would be as a father and mother to her in their care, advice, and counsel for the good of her soul, and also to be a help and guide to her in the choice of a fit match for her when she is capable or inclined to so great a change of her condition, that the blessing of the Lord may go along with it.

[*Unexpected Claimants Disposed Of*]

It may be there is some other of my friends or kindred or acquaintance that I might have expressed my love unto had they come into my memory. I have endeavored what I can to forget none, but being forgotten, I hope they will not be offended nor take it unkindly at my hands. For I would not willingly forget my relations nor show myself unthankful to any to whom I am beholden for former courtesies or engagements real. Therefore, my will is that if at any time or times hereafter within the space of twelve months or two years at most after my decease any person or persons whatsoever in Old England or New by virtue or by reason of kin or consanguinity to me now not known or at least not remembered may or can claim to have any lawful interest into or benefit of any estate of mine by reason thereof and do lawfully produce and prove the same, then to such of them as shall so do my mind and will is that my executor, whom I shall hereafter name, shall pay unto the same person or persons so lawfully claiming any benefit by reason as aforesaid the sum of ten shillings apiece which I do hereby give them to cut off any further claim of, in, or to the estate of me, the said testator. And likewise my mind and will is that if any of my said legatees shall not be contented with the legacies by me given to them but shall by any means prove vexatious or troublesome to my executor, my will is that they and every one of them so molesting or vexing shall lose and forfeit their several or respectful legacies to the use of my executor.

[*His Son, Executor and Residual Legatee*]

Item. I give and bequeath unto my loving son Major Benjamin Keayne all the rest and residue of my estate whatsoever, movable or immovable, that I have or shall not bequeath in this will, and also all those legacies bequeathed that shall not be paid by the death or removal of any of the legatees before the time of the legacies payable grow due or any overplus of my estate not disposed of, to the aforenamed Benjamin Keayne, whom I make, ordain, appoint, and by these present constitute to be my full and sole executor of this my last will and testament. And I do desire that all occasions of difference or discontent or falling out betwixt his mother and he may carefully be avoided and that all things about my estate may be carried on in love and sweet agreement as betwixt a loving mother and a dutiful son, and that they lay no unnecessary burdens each upon the other, but that my son as a dutiful child may ease his mother in what he can and free her from any distractions in settling that part of my estate bequeathed to her [so that] it may be to her best ease, supply, and comfort during her life, and with all expedition to gather in my debts which at my death shall be due unto me (which are a considerable part of my estate) and to take a just inventory and valuation of all things that I shall leave behind me. Everything that is sold is to be put away to the best advantage so that my legacies may neither be unpaid nor curtailed contrary to my true intent, there appearing sufficient estate to do it if well ordered and improved. For that end I have given two years time and some more for the doing of it, because I know it cannot well be comfortably performed without some hazard or danger to my estate in a shorter time.

[*His Records, Files, and Accounts: Testimonies of a Worthy Life*]

And as a good help hereunto I advise that my shop books, debt books, and all my books of account may carefully be looked up, kept together and diligently perused, seeing that almost everything which belongs to my estate is by myself committed to writing in one book or other, either in my day book of what I buy or sell, or in my debt book, of which there is chiefly three in use, namely, one bound in brown vellum which I call vellum debt book, the other bound in thin parchment, which I call the new debt book, the third is bound in white vellum, which I keep constantly in my closet at Boston and is called my book of creditor and debitor, in which is the sum of most of my accounts contracted wherein there is accounts between myself and others with the accounts balanced on either side and also an account of my adventures by shipping with their returns and also an account of what debts I owe and how far they are discharged.

There is also in my closet a long paper book bound in white parchment which I call my inventory book, in which I do yearly (commonly) cast up my whole estate. It is a breviate of my whole estate from year to year and shows how the Lord is pleased either to increase or decrease my estate from year to year. This will be of special use and concernment to my executors and overseers to direct them in their proceedings about my estate, there being in it the valuation of my estate from time to time except household stuff, movable goods, and such things, and wherein and in what the chief part of my estate lies. In this book you will find a particular account of what debts I myself owe to any at the time of my casting up, and also what was at that time owing to me from others and by whom which I use to draw briefly out of all my other debt books into that. [It contains] also an account of such debts as I account desperate or doubtful, which I place by themselves and do make them no part of my estate though some of them will be got in; and [also] what debts I account good, either in Old England or New, whether by book or bill. All or the most of the debts by bills you shall find under the debitors' hands together in a box in my cabinet, which stands in my closet at Boston, in the middle or biggest box therein. Some other bills and accounts are in my leather letter case which commonly lies upon my table in that closet.

There is also divers accounts and debts that are kept in several sheets of paper at my farm which chiefly belongs to my farm and accounts there. They are debts of the iron works and the neighbors thereabouts for things trusted from my farm. These had need to be carefully looked up, kept together from losing, and perused because they are all in loose papers and not in a book. These papers I keep in my trunk within my closet at the farm.

Now in that inventory book before mentioned is also set down the particulars of my estate in housing, lands, rents, debts, cattle of all sorts, farms, with some plate, jewels, and some particular chief things with their several prices and valuations, with a particular of all the wares and commodities and corn, either in my closet, warehouses, cellars, garret, corn-lofts both at Boston and at my farm or anywhere else, that I had to sell at the time of my casting up, with the names, quantities, prices, and sorts of them all. [It also contains] a particular of the charges that I have been at yearly in building, housekeeping, apparel, servants, and workmen's wages both at my farm and at Boston, and [also] whether I gained or lost by my estate that year and how much.

Only this caution and direction is to be taken notice of in that book [regarding] the debts that I myself owe to any man. I set them down to the full where I know certainly either by reckoning and agreement or by bills what they are. For other debts that I owe which depends upon reckonings and accounts between us, they having had some things upon account of me and I of them and we have not had opportunity to examine and settle the account between us to know justly what is due—in such cases, where I can but guess, there I commonly charge myself with the most and over rather than under. And for the debts that is due to me from others and do depend upon my reckonings and accounts between us and so the exact debt is not, therefore, certainly known at that time, I do usually charge them in that book or put them down less than my full due (unless they be in bills in which there can be no denial or just exception of controversy in).

Also in that book I charge some debts under the head of doubtful or desperate debts. Not that they are all so in their own nature, for many of them I have got in myself and others may now also be gotten in or part of them. For if I looked at them as utterly desperate I would not trouble that book with the mention of them. Therefore, they have some life in them and [are] to be gotten in, in part or in whole, for I see by experience that some debts that I have looked at as quite lost in 3 or 4 years after have proved good and many other that have been ancient debts have in some place or other in that book brought them to account. I do not every year post them over anew as being hopeless but only take out here and there some if there appear to be any new life or hope in them. This course I take because I would not delude myself in making my estate show the greater by bringing all debts or bad debts into account as a good estate when they are not like so to prove. But when any of them are got in they are an addition to the estate more than before was accounted upon. So also for them that are there placed under the name and head of good debts, when you come to receive your pay, you are not to look in this book [under] what is there [called] full and just debt, but to turn to their account in the debt books, where the time and particulars of all things they had and the prices agreed upon are set down or to the bills under their own hands.

Amongst these accounts and debts at my farm before mentioned, which are kept only in loose papers, [there] are many of them not put into any of my debt books and therefore are to be kept as carefully as my other bills or debt books. There is a particular account of all my cattle and other things and what increase comes of them from year to year, which of them I sell away or kill for my own use, and also which of them dies by casualty or are lost by the wolves, and how many remains of all sorts every year, with their ages, prices, and worth taken every spring or beginning of the new year. By this you will see what living cattle I have, of oxen, cows, calves, horses, swine, and in whose hands they are, to require them. In this also, I do used to set down the value of the cattle at less than they are worth and than they would yield if I were to sell them or to put them off one by one. There is also the particulars of my farm and the value of it. These, with the inventory book of my estate before mentioned, will be a good direction and great help to you when you come to take an inventory of my estate and to value the particulars thereof.

There is also at my farm a long paper book bound in parchment, such a one as my inventory book in my closet at Boston which I mentioned before. This book I commonly keep in that room at my farm which I keep locked up for my own use. In it is the particulars of the charges and profits that I make of my farm every year, with an account of the corn and apples and butter and cheese that is made, and where they are, with some debts therein due to me, and some other accounts [which are] to be kept and perused.

There is at my farm also many printed books both great and small, divinity, history, military books, that I made use of there, and some written sermon books, both in my closet and chamber there. There is also some plate, [such] as a silver porringer, a sack bowl, a silver hot water cup, 3 silver spoons that were kept for our own use there in a little box in my closet. There is also in my standish at the farm, which hath a lock and key to it, some silver and peage[6] in one of the private or secret boxes of the same, which I keep in my closet there. And these things are besides all the bedding, sheets, linen, household stuff, dairy vessels, carts, etc.

There is also at Boston a long paper book bound in parchment kept in the closet there which is called a receipt book of moneys that I have paid from time to time, especially when they come home to receive their money. Not that we take receipts for all we pay in that book. Sometimes I take receipts upon the bill of account and also for moneys paid abroad; we take them in papers and keep them upon files. This book is carefully to be kept as well as those papers that are filed up, because it may clear some things as doubts or objections that may come about debts long since that have been paid by me. Had this book been lost I had been in great danger to have paid 200 lb. twice over, which I have mentioned before in this will, but that after long search amongst many books and papers I found the receipt of it in this book, being before utterly denied that it was ever paid.

There is another book upon the table in my closet at Boston bound in leather in octavo which I call my pocket book. This is carefully to be preserved and perused. In it is a particular account of my daily or weekly expenses and charges for diet, apparel, and housekeeping, which is summed up every week from year to year and what every week's charge amounts to. This will give light to many things, [such] as what is paid to bakers, butchers, shops, carting of wood, rates, and divers such charges to several

[6] I.e., wampum.

persons possible some of which may be demanded again when I am dead. [Such things] this book, compared with their own accounts in my debt book, will easily clear. And if any debt should be demanded of my executors which I have not made myself debtor for in some of my account books or charged in that inventory book, except it should be some debt that hath been made since the time of the last casting up of my estate, it may be justly suspected and the truth of it to be questioned. For I am as careful to charge myself with what I owe as what is owing to me, and usually once a year I draw out in a sheet of paper (which you may find amongst other loose sheets of accounts in my closet at Boston) all the debts that I can call to mind that I owe to any man, so that I may take care to pay them. And in this drawing them out of my other books I place them all together in these yearly papers.

There is 2 other books bound up in vellum in my closet at Boston which I call number books. These were of use when I kept shop in London and here but are not now, as you may see by the date and things contained in them, of any use now. You will meet with some other old debt books [such] as one at the farm bound in leather in folio, and others there and at home in parchment, in which you will find [that] many debts stand uncrossed. I suppose by the alphabets or in the margin against these debts you will find them posted or transferred into other debt books of a later date, [such] as the three debt books first mentioned, [unless] they be such debts that I have little hope to get in. You will also find in my closet at Boston a paper book bound up in vellum of quarto, which was sent me from London by my son Mr. Gray and my brother Jupe who had the care of receiving the rents of the 3 children of my sister so long as the leases lasted, and who was sub-executor to my sister's will in my stead. This book contains only the accounts belonging to the 3 children, Anthony, Mary, and Benjamin Jupe, in which is mentioned what money they have received in England ever since my sister's death, what they have laid out of it for the lord's quit rents, towards repairing the houses, and other charges there, and what they have sent over to me of it towards the charge of their maintenance here. It is needful to have it safe kept, though there be the less use of it now because I have reckoned with Anthony and Mary Jupe and gave them an account of what I had received and laid out for them, which account was examined and perused by 2 or 3 friends on the children's choice and behalf and I have received general releases and discharges from them which are amongst my bills in my cabinet and in another box that my cabinet stands upon. There is only now Benjamin to reckon withal when he comes to age, but he will owe me more than his brother or sister, for, by reason of his lameness and continual sickness, I was at greater charge with him than with either of them, having laid out 60 or 70 lb. for him more than I received till his legacies and rents given him by his Uncle Jupe came to be due to him, as you may see in his account in the vellum debt book.

There is also in my closet at Boston a long white box upon which my cabinet stands, which is full of accounts, reckonings, and releases between me and others, with some bills and bonds and receipts for purchase of lands and other things of long standing which I have always carefully kept by me to have recourse to when there hath been need of clearing things done or paid long since. Sometimes I have had special occasion to search over [these accounts;] and so may you possibly if anything should be brought into question of such kinds when I am dead.

All these books and accounts and writings I mention in this my will the more particularly that my executor especially and my overseers may call for them, find them all out, take special care for the safe keeping of them, and peruse them diligently. For if any one of them should be lost or conveyed away you would be at a great loss and much to seek in my accounts; and it may prove a great loss to my estate. Of the like use are many other written papers and books in my closet there in loose sheets together, and therefore to be perused and kept, some of which though they be evened and quite discharged long ago and crossed [out] yet I keep them by me that if any wrangling person pretending ignorance should call things to an account again as some have done, by having recourse to those books and papers I can show them when and how and in what it was discharged and evened. Therefore, very few of those papers are to be neglected or cast by as if they were kept for no use at all.

And when all these books and writings, not only of debts and accounts and worldly business but also of divinity, sermon books, and some of military discipline and exercise and of merchandise and divers other occasions which I have writ with my own hand, and divers other writings which are not now extant, besides all that I have read and done while I kept shop and since, with the care and toil of my farm,—if all these should be of no other use, yet they will testify to the world on my behalf that I have not lived an idle, lazy, or dronish life, nor spent my time wantonly, fruitlessly or in company-keeping as some have been too ready to asperse me, or that I have had in my whole time either in Old England or New many spare hours to spend unprofitably away or to refresh myself with recreations, except reading and writing hath been a recreation to me, which sometimes is mixed with pain and labor enough. Rather I have studied and endeavored to redeem my time as a thing most dear and precious to me and have often denied myself in such refreshings that otherwise I might lawfully have made use of. And therefore it were well if man were less censorious of other men's lives and actions and more watchful over their own lest they speak evil out of some private grudge of things they know not.

And happy yea more happy would it have been for me if I had been as careful and as exact in keeping an account of my sins and the debts I owe to God and of that spiritual estate between God and my own soul and that I could as easily have made it appear to others or to myself when I gained or when I lost and to have taken as much pains this way as in the other, which, though I cannot truly say I have altogether neglected or omitted, yet comparatively I may justly say I have been greatly deficient in that one thing necessary. But I hope the Lord in mercy will not impute it but freely pardon all my negligences this way in the Lord Jesus Christ and for His sake only.

[Emergency Provisions]

And because it may possibly fall out that my son who is my executor may be out of this country (as now he is) at the time of my death, therefore if it should so prove, my desire is that my loving brother Mr. John Wilson, pastor of Boston, would be pleased to stand in my son's room as his substitute, or to desire my cousin Mr. Edward Rawson, secretary, or Lionel Johnson, our deacon, or some other sufficient, godly, able man that he shall appoint or approve of to be assistant to my loving wife, Mrs. Anne Keayne, and to transact all the business of an executor till my son may be sent for and come in person to take charge of it himself. [Just such a] service I did willingly perform for my brother Wilson when his brother, Doctor Wilson, died, himself being in this country, and for this kindness not only myself but my son and wife (I doubt not) will acknowledge their thankfulness. And if it should please God that my son would be dead before or die in coming, for so it may possibly fall out, then my will and appointment is that my loving wife should be sole executrix of this my last will and testament during the time of her widowhood and no longer, and to see all things performed herein according to my intent and her uttermost ability, with the assistance and advice of my brother Wilson (as before I have expressed), whose help and faithfulness herein I much depend upon to see all things carried on right and straight, and also by the help of the rest of my overseers, or the greatest part of them.

And my desire and charge is to my executor and my wife, in case she should be, or otherwise so far as in her lieth, that they be faithful and punctual in the discharge of this my will to the uttermost of their abilities and to prevent all objections [that] the estate falls short or that I have given away more than my estate will be able to make good. For I would not willingly have [any] that I bequeath anything unto if they be alive or in this country when their legacies grow due, nor any public use that I have given ought to, to be defrauded or disappointed of it contrary to my true intent upon any seeming pretenses, as it is usual with many executors to the great dishonor of those that have betrusted them with their estates, ... [unless] it should manifestly and clearly appear to my overseers chiefly or any other honest and understanding men that it is not fraud but some clear and apparent loss that is befallen my estate, either by desperate debts which before I accounted good, by loss at sea, or fire, or by fall of cattle, land, or other commodities in the country, or some other unexpected providence or change of things here not yet foreseen between the time of my making this will and my death or before my legacies are to be performed.

Therefore, my will is if some such loss should come of it to no considerable value, that my executor should bear it out of his part [in case] the overplus of my estate not bequeathed should not do it, [even] though he have somewhat the less for himself, [unless] his own part and legacies fall short also by some such considerable loss. But if there should be any such manifest change and loss in my estate, then my will is that all my legacies should bear a proportionable share in that loss by way of abatement as they are paid or by the omitting wholly of such gifts as are to some public uses which shall be judged by my executor and overseers to be of least concernment and may best be spared. For if I had found my estate to be less than I esteemed it to be, I should have given less both to my executor and in other gifts and legacies.

[Principles of Giving, Reviewed]

... My opinion and judgment hath been and still is, not only before God had blessed me with a large and comfortable estate but since also, that in point of disposing a man's outward estate, especially if it were of any value and his children not very numerous, I look at it as a great oversight and evil to give all or the most part of a large estate only to wife and children to make them great or rich in the world and to leave little or nothing to friends or to any public or charitable use [even] though there be great occasion and necessities of it and some poor afflicted Josephs that cry for help. For as it is the Lord out of His free bounty that gives us our estates, be they more or less (for it is not our own hands' diligence or wisdom but His blessing only that makes rich) so He may justly challenge a part and interest in the same; and also the commonwealth or place where we live and where we have got more or less of that estate is also to be considered.

I think wife and children ought to have so much as whereby they may be enabled to live comfortably, to be preserved from outward straits and snares proportionable to that estate that God hath bestowed upon the husband or parents. For I do not think that others should be eased and they grieved and.straitened, or that they should be forgot when others are remembered. For God appoints [that] we should first provide for our own family with a wise and careful hand therein according to the love, respect, and dutiful carriage of wife and children and the hopes they give of a staid and gracious conversation, remembering still that God and the country should come in for a child's part in our estates, also in some reasonable proportion suitable to the extent thereof, lest the Lord blast and take away all from those to whom it is given. And as I think dutiful and loving wives and children should be taken care of in the first place before others and be comfortably provided for, so I think all is too much that is given to vexatious, prodigal, imperious wives or rebellious, undutiful, and spendthrift children.

Therefore, my care hath been in making this my will with the best wisdom and understanding that God hath bestowed upon me so to provide that I may not wrong my son (having but one child and one that I do love and have cause tenderly to respect) nor my wife, . . . nor legatees, but so to give that all may be performed without just cause of complaint, prejudice, or loss to any. Neither would I make a great show of gifts to friends and to public and charitable uses and perform little or nothing if God himself disappoint not, lest some should approach me with an affectation and vainglory. But how it can justly be imputed to me, seeing those things are to be performed when I am dead and in my grave and therefore not capable of being puffed up with pride or outward applause (for what good will the praises of men do to me when I am not? —and considering also that neither man nor women now living hath neither seen or read this will or any one line of it that I know of or of my former will made 4 or 5 years before this) I see not. Neither have I made known what my purpose or intent is this way or what I have done herein to any man living that they should trumpet out my praise beforehand, but have kept all private in my own breast and have done or desire to do that which God alone hath inclined my heart unto. And had I made my purposes herein known I doubt not but I should have met with discouragements enough and with advice and persuasions to alter many things herein. Yet peradventure at last I shall not want reproaches from some of want of discretion, if not worse, for what I have done, though I aim at good in all. And if they should, I suppose their reproaches will not much hurt me.

But if I did not see and believe that there is sufficient in my estate to discharge all that I have given away and to spare with some addition to my son over and above his third part according to my best judgment and valuation, I would judge myself of folly and indiscretion and would presently alter it. But I am very much deceived in my account and the estimate of my estate if besides [all] that I have given away there be not a liberal provision made both for my wife and my son to live comfortably upon, yea, and to my son a good deal above a third part of my whole estate, especially when God shall please to take away his mother and her third return back again to him, or so much of it as I have appointed in this will before. [If not,] I must needs say I have showed little care and wisdom therein, yea, and do hereby declare it to be quite contrary to my true intent and will in that particular . . . to put my executor or wife to all the care, pains, cost, and trouble in looking to and selling or putting off my estate and paying to everyone else their legacies and themselves to be at last deceived or disappointed of their due, or that others should be fully paid their legacies and those which both in nature and religion I do and ought to esteem most should fall short in theirs or be forced to take it in the worst or most unvendible part of my estate, and others that to me are but strangers in comparison (though I look at them as loving and Christian friends) should be paid first or in the best of what I have.

[A Breviate of the Main Provisions]

Therefore, [my desire is] to clear all things and to make my intentions as plain as I can, not having fully expressed it before as I remember. . . . My full meaning is this: when my funeral charges and debts (which I hope then will not be many, for at this time they are but very little exceeding one hundred pounds if so much) are paid or so much set apart or accounted for out of my estate as will pay them (or else the rest cannot properly be called a great estate if any debts lie upon it unprovided for), . . . I appoint the remainder, when inventoried and valued as equally as may be to be divided . . . into 3 equal parts. My clear estate according to my best judgment and valuation and as I found it at the last casting up and settling of my estate which was done this spring, one thousand six hundred fifty and three (the debts that myself owed either in Old

England or New and my desperate or doubtful debts being left out and not brought into the account of my estate as you may see in that long book called the inventory book of my estate in anno 1653) . . . I found to be worth four thousand pounds or thereabout, and I think I have overvalued nothing. Yea in many things I know I could make much more of them if I were now to sell them. Though possibly I may be a little mistaken in some other things, yet I conceive one thing compared with another all will amount to my valuation, if not exceed it.[7]

Now this estate, as I said before, I would have divided into three parts. The one third part thereof . . . I give to my executor, Major Benjamin Keayne, both in lands and goods. The second third part of my estate, be it a thousand pounds or more, I take wholly to myself, to be at my own disposing, and to give the same away wholly amongst my friends and for public and pious uses. In [this portion,] as I said before, God and the country and my own part lies, and out of it I have given away by this will in certain legacies, besides the accidental ones that may happen, about a thousand and two hundred pounds as I cast it up, which, for ought I see, my estate will well bear without wronging either my executor or my wife or offering any unkindness to them. If I thought that either of them should apprehend otherwise I would not have done for them nor provided so liberally on their behalf as I have done, for I know what power I have to dispose of my own estate and if their parts should have proved far less I think they ought to have been contented. Therefore, I hope they will not dislike nor be offended at what I have given away to others nor think I have been too profuse, [unless] some of those uses that I have given to may be thought to be less necessary or better have been spared than given to, though I was not of that mind when I did it.

Now there yet remains one third part of my estate clear or within a small matter [of it,] out of which my wife is to be provided for, unto whom I have given the third part of all my lands, housing, tenements, namely the profits of them, to improve and enjoy to her best benefit and use as long as she lives. This I doubt not will afford a large and comfortable living to her and some overplus above her expenses to lay up every year whereby she may have somewhat to distribute amongst her friends when she dies. This third, how much soever it proves, when the Lord shall be pleased to remove her out of this world, I have given the one-half

---

[7] Keayne's repeated insistence that he was not giving away more than he comfortably could was in vain. He substantially overestimated his estate. It was officially appraised at his death in 1656 at £2569 19s. 3d., a sum insufficient to cover his bequests. Suffolk County Probate Records, III. 160–173; Morgan, "A Boston Heiress," 503–504.

thereof to my son and heir, Benjamin Keayne; the other half of it I have equally divided between my grandchild, Hannah Keayne, and the College at Cambridge, in case my son should have no other children, as legacies of my love to them above what else I had given to them. By this account it may easily appear that I have taken care for my wife and son, and that though I have given away much in gifts as well to them as to others, yet I have not given away to the full latitude of the remaining part of my estate, much less above it or beyond it if I have not much mistaken.

Now having given this account of the equity of my proceedings in this will of mine and in the disposing of that estate which the Lord in goodness hath been pleased to bestow upon me, and as I am bound both by grace and nature first to provide for my own, viz., for those that are nearest to me (as I have said before) and then for those that are further off, therefore, my will is that my son may first take his third part out of my lands, houses, cattle, money, plate, or any sort of household stuff or any other goods that he best likes of, according to the value given to him, he allowing as much in account for them as any other man would give for the same if they were to buy them. Then next my wife is to have her third part in lands and tenements, and if she desire to have a cow or two, a piece of plate or two, or any other part of the household stuff besides what I have given her as a legacy (and her own peculiar wearing apparel, which I think is not equal to be valued or brought into the inventory of my estate, nor Hannah Keayne's neither) I desire that she may have it, she giving as much as others would do for the same and paying for it either to some of those that I have given legacies unto or else by taking so much less as that she desires to buy will come to in her land and housing with a consideration and allowance that may equalize the difference between lands and goods. The land is all to be returned at her death, but the goods so bought will be her own to dispose of as she pleaseth without returning them back again, so that my estate may receive no loss that way. If any other or just way can be thought of between my overseers and she I shall leave it to them.

Next to be set apart [is] that which shall be judged most fit for what I have given to Hannah Keayne for her portion and to be kept either in her father's hands if he desire it or to any other [person] or other way that it may be best improved to her advantage according to my will. And this [is] to be taken out of such part of my estate, cattle, or goods as may be most useful to make her pay good.

Next to hers, the legacies that I have given to my cousin Mary Morse and Anthony and Benjamin Jupe, her brothers, . . . may be set apart and provided for according to my will.

Next to them, . . . my brother and sister Wilson with their children, as I have mentioned in my will, may be taken care of.

Next or indeed next after Hannah Keayne I desire my executor would as soon as with conveniency he can take care to pay my loving friends that I have sequestered to be overseers of this my will, to their content, unto whom not only myself, son, and wife shall be most beholden to for the pains and care they will be put unto but all others that have gifts and legacies bequeathed unto them in this will.

Now these things premised, the difficulty that I know not well how to get over . . . which I desire may wisely be taken care of by my overseers and provided against is this: I suppose all my good debts, my cattle, household stuff, and movables, or the best and most vendible parts of them will but pay (or but little over) the legacies and gifts that I have given away, and then there will remain not much more than my housing at Boston, my farm, and some other lands to my son and wife. Now if he should pay all my living stock away in legacies the farm will be disenabled and unprovided in stock and so the more unfit to let out. If he should pay away all the household stuff and movables, then my housing would be left naked and he little to live upon but a dead stock and so through necessity be forced to put away some of my land or part of my housing at an undervalue for his own supply and maintenance. And though land be the more certain and will afford yearly rents, yet I look at it as the deadest estate and that which yields least profit considering the value or worth of it, though the chiefest part of my estate lies in it. Now my chief aim and desire is, in all that I have done, that my son may have an estate upon which he may live comfortably and out of debt and so to preserve and carry on that estate with credit amongst his neighbors and be enabled to do good with it, and so also my wife. Therefore, whether to part with some of the land and some of the housing to pay legacies and gifts and to keep for his own estate some of the chief of the household stuff and of the living stock in which there is great hazard by death and wolves—on that I know not what to advise [so] that my will may be accomplished and yet my son put into a comfortable capacity of an honorable and comfortable maintenance without throwing himself into straits or bringing himself into debt in paying the legacies otherwise that so he might preserve his inheritance free.

And I am the less able to give advice herein because I know not what course my son's spirit or inclination will lead him to follow, whether farming, grazing, merchandising, or trading, or to let out all and lead a more private life and live only upon his rents and estate; whether he intends to live here, which I chiefly desire and would enjoin him to, if it be not greatly and apparently to his prejudice [unless] times here should much change and grow worse, where he may enjoy God and His ordinances and good company; or whether he should have any purpose to remove at all. Which way being uncertain, I know not how to advise about his estate for the best. Yet considering that my own debts are small and nothing of necessity to be paid presently except my funeral charges, the legacies not payable [for] two years [unless] he wills [it] himself and some of them a good while after, as the will shows, I should think it no hard matter if wisely ordered to pay the most of these legacies in two or three years out of the rents of the houses, the increase of the cattle, the crops of corn at the farm, with the other improvements of such an estate, and keep the main stock of cattle, the most of the goods and household stuff and the land and housing entire. The debts which is owing to me will also be a good help hereunto. I would make no great question through God's blessing to do it myself and not weaken or impair my main estate very little if at all. Howsoever, I have made choice of wise, skillful, and godly overseers that will be able to direct him herein. Unto them my earnest request and desire is that they would be pleased to consider, advise, and assist my son and wife according to the best of their judgments and apprehensions how to accomplish my will in that manner that their estates may be preserved and not spoiled or sunk in the discharge hereof. For it is meet that what I have given and do intend for them may not be lessened nor diminished, though legacies and gifts should abate somewhat if there should be just occasion, which now cannot be foreseen and provided for at so large a distance, not knowing what may happen or fall out at such a time.

[Objections Removed: Oppression in His Calling]

Now having thus cleared my intentions plainly and really in all things as far as I can remember, which hath occasioned my will to be far larger than I either intended or desired, there are 2 or 3 objections which doth lie in the way, which being answered or removed I shall draw to an end. For I desire in this my will to give an account of my actions and endeavor to remove all jealousies as near as I can, these being as it were my last words that will live to speak for me when I am dead and in my grave. And God may be pleased so far to bless something or other that I have had occasion to express in this will, that such which have taken liberty to load me with divers reproaches and long to lay me under a dark cloud may have cause to see that they have done amiss and now to be sorry for it, though they have not been so before.

The objections are these:

First, if I value my estate to be worth 4000 lb. or thereabouts, how could I get such an estate with a good conscience or without oppression in my calling, seeing it is known to some that I had no portion from my parents or friends to begin the world withal. If none did know of this I am bound to acknowledge [it,] that all may be attributed to the free mercy and kindness of God alone who raiseth up and pulleth down as He pleaseth, so that when I call to mind my first beginning or my first going to London I may with old Jacob thankfully say, with my staff came I over this Jordan and now the Lord hath given me two bands.

To which I answer, I have now traded for myself about 40 or 50 years and through the favor of God, though I had very little at first to begin with, yet I had good credit and good esteem and respect in the place where I lived so that I did ever drive a great trade not only since I came hither but especially in England.

Now to get 4000 lb. in 40 or 50 years is not 100 lb. a year clear gains, one year with another, which we account to be no great matter in driving but a small trade by an industrious and provident man, especially where there is no great trusting of chapmen or giving of credit which usually is subject to great hazards and losses. A tradesman or merchant that hath a full trade may get a 100 lb. a year above his expenses and a great deal more very honestly without hurting his own conscience or wronging those that he deals with at all.

Since I came into New England it is well known to some that I brought over with me two or 3000 lb. in good estate of my own, and I have been here in a way of trade and merchandise besides farming now this 18 years. He that hath a stock of his own of 2 or 3000 lb. to manage in a way of trade, I think he may very lawfully and honestly get 200 lb. a year by it clear if his expenses be not very great and large. And yet with turning and managing this stock of my own (besides what goods have been sent me from England by other men to a considerable value from time to time) I have not cleared near 100 lb. a year above my expenses since I came hither, which is not 5 lb. per cent clear gains. And yet I have been no prodigal spender as I have been no niggardly sparer in things needful, as the account of my daily and weekly expenses will testify for me when those books come to be viewed over, whether ... [in] relation to my expenses in Old England or since I came hither.

For ... I have undergone many censures since I came hither according to men's uncharitable and various apprehensions, some looking at me as an oppressor in trading and getting unconscionably by what I sold and others as covetous and niggardly in housekeeping and not so liberal and bountiful as I should be. How those two contraries can justly be charged upon me and yet have increased my estate no more in so long a time I yet see not, [unless] it be [charged] by such as care not what they say of other men though never so false, so [long as] they may lay others under reproach and magnify themselves and their ways by disgracing of others. But it is nothing for me to be judged of men. I have labored to bear it with patience and to approve my heart and ways to God that judgeth righteously. Yet these things hath made me the more willing to clear myself in all material things in this my last testament. Though it be somewhat contrary to the nature of a will, yet I am willing to leave this upon public record as a just defense for myself, knowing that a will will be read and made known and may be perused, searched, or copied out by any when other writings will be more hid and obscured. And then let not my words only but my real actions bear witness for me or against me in the hearts of all that are willing to judge indifferently and without prejudice, whether I have justly deserved what here I have undergone, either by words or actions. The whole passages of my life in all my dealings since I was a prentice is to be found in one book or another written with my own hand upon one occasion or another, which, though before hath been kept secret to myself, yet now will be exposed to the view of others and their censure when they will be perused after my death.

[Objections Removed: Evasion of Taxes]

But some may further object [that] if I do value my estate at so much as before mentioned how could I deal honestly in suffering myself to be valued in rates to the country but after a 1000 lb. estate at most, or sometimes less.

To which I answer, first, that I do not think a man is bound in conscience to make known his whole estate and suffer himself to be valued to the uttermost extent thereof if he can honestly prevent it. It is not so in any nation in the world that I have heard or read of, except in case of great extremity by an enemy in the country or at the walls when all is in hazard to be lost, but quite contrary. In England I have known knights, aldermen, merchants worth many thousands and have had lands worth some hundred pounds a year known, and yet to subsidies and public charges are not valued at half their estates. Many reasons may be given why it should not be otherwise.

I know myself and others here pay more to rates and public charges yearly than those that are 3 times of my estate in England in 4 or 5 years. What charges they are at now is not the question nor to be propounded as an example to us, because our condition and theirs is not alike. But for myself, all the while I stayed in England I was never rated but after 3 lb. goods, and at last 4 lb., to any subsidy. And yet sometimes we had not a subsidy in 8 or 10 years granted. Here we are rated every year, and in some one year I have paid near 20 lb. to country rates. Therefore, though some may judge that men's estates are undervalued, everyone seeking to ease themselves and lay the burden upon others, yet rates did rise so high upon the pound and came so fast about that men may be truly said in that respect to be rated for above and beyond their estates.

When my estate was taken as others were I could not say upon safe and just grounds that it was never so much as now it is, being much in debt myself (which now through great mercy I have well overcome and discharged) and having many debts owing to me, both in Old England and New, the most of which might have miscarried as some hath done, besides some adventures I had at sea of a considerable value which none can reckon as a sure and safe estate till God brings back the returns, as we find by sad experience and loss.

Lastly, the most part of my estate now lies in my farm, in cattle, houses, and household stuff, which in rating are never valued to the uttermost worth to no man (household stuff not at all, seeing that turns to no profit but are impaired by daily use). As for housing, there would appear some kind of injustice and inequality if they should be rated high, being chiefly for entertainment, drawing charges by the accommodating of others and also are chargeable to keep in repair and are but harbors for themselves and others. Now neither God nor any Christian state in policy would have their inhabitants crushed or weakened by continual charge but so that they may be nourished and preserved in a thriving condition, that they may live well and be still able to do good in their places for the carrying on of public charges. Besides, now the Court hath taken up another and more equal way of rating men, and that is, by their visible estates and an easy and equal imposition thereon, as 1 d. in every 20 s. they have in good estate. By this no man's conscience is racked by questions and answers or by an injunction for every man to bring in a just account of the full value of his estate, which hath proved a temptation to me. Against this way I think none can justly except or complain, as I conceive, except such as have no estate but what is visible and yet are much in debt and have nothing but that visible estate to pay it with and yet nothing is abated them for their debts. Such, then, are rated above their estates.

[Possible Attacks on the Estate]

But some possibly will object, further, what if some expressions in your will should prove offensive and some, pretending exceptions (you having many enemies that will be ready to take any advantage against you), should complain to the Court against it where things may be so aggravated out of prejudice that some fine may be procured and imposed upon you and so to take away part of that estate which you think you have left secure to your son, wife, and friends.

I answer, first, I know no just cause of offense that I have given in any expressions herein that malice itself can take advantage of [unless] they should be wrested contrary to my true intent and meaning. And if any will do so, no man can express himself so warily but some wits may make use of to a man's prejudice and make that appear to be evil which is good or harmless in itself, as I have seen and known by many experiences and sad examples in my lifetime, and that both for words and actions, as many can remember as well as myself.

I confess that I have known and seen such practices in Old England that when some chief ones have had desire to fish away a part of a dying man's estate they have taken exceptions against his will or quarreled either with some expressions or gifts mentioned therein to cast the fairer gloss upon their corrupt practice and project, though it could not be so hid. And many here knows how deeply many have suffered, both in the Star Chamber and High Commission Court, for good actions and speeches interpreted quite contrary to the true meaning thereof. But I hope that neither I nor mine shall live to see such practices creep in or be countenanced in our Court. Doubtless the times would be strangely changed if any such thing should come to pass here that men should be made transgressors for a harmless word.

If any such thing should be urged and brought against me to my prejudice, who or what will they fine? I am gone and estate of my own I have none left, no more than will bring me to my grave. I have given away all, if not more than all. And if there were a just offense given by me, or not justly taken up by others, it were not just to take away any part of the wife's or children's portions for the father's or husband's offense, they being no ways accessory to it.

If there were any estate of mine left undisposed of upon which a fine might be laid, what will they do with it if levied? If it should be to gratify any private man, that would appear too gross; if for the public or commonwealth, there might be some pretense if I had bequeathed nothing that way. But having given away so large a part of my estate to public uses (so much that many a wiser man having such or a better estate than mine would not have given half so much from his wife, children, and friends as I have done, and possibly I shall be reproached of folly by many, I doubt not of some, for this I have done) therefore in such a case it will be more honorable for the public that my will should stand inviolable (the will of the dead usually having been held sacred) than for any man upon any pretense to seek by power to alter or infringe it.

Lastly, though I fear no such thing nor see any just cause or ground that any can have for such an apprehension, yet because I know not how strangely things may alter nor who may get into places of power and authority between this and the time of my death, nor what pretenses corrupt or prejudiced men may make, therefore if any should be active this way and promote any such complaint against me or my will when I am dead and gone and can neither answer nor suffer for myself, with any intent either to get any part of my estate away if I had any left or any part of that estate which I have given away to my son, wife, or any other mentioned in this will, or shall be troublesome or vexatious to my executor on pretense of any fault or offense of mine, and it be entertained or countenanced, then my will is and I do hereby declare it to be my will and full mind, that all and every gift or legacy that is mentioned in this will to be laid out and disposed of for any general or public use, whether for library, granary, armory, courthouse, school, or college, market house, etc., save only that hundred and twenty pounds that I have given to the school and poor in Boston and what other legacies that I have given to particular friends or persons . . . shall utterly cease and become void and of no effect to the uses and behoof of the things and purposes before mentioned, and shall be disposed of as I shall hereafter appoint and mention.

My will is that out of those forementioned general or public gifts that are to cease, my loving wife, Mrs. Anne Keayne, may have one hundred pounds thereof to her own particular use and benefit.

And my will further is that one hundred pounds more of those gifts be equally divided between my sister's three children, Anthony Jupe,

Benjamin Jupe, that lives with myself, and Mary Jupe, now Mary Morse. And if any of them shall die before they come to receive their parts, then that part to go to the survivors of them.

Item. I will and bequeath further out of the aforementioned gifts ceasing and becoming void upon any such occasion as is before mentioned one hundred pounds more thereof to my grandchild Hannah Keayne, to be paid to her either at the day of her marriage or when she comes to that age as is before mentioned in other legacies that I have given to her.

Item. I will and bequeath one hundred pounds more of the said gifts to be divided amongst my kindred in Old England: as to the wife of my brother John Keayne that did live in Chesham not far from London, if she shall be then alive, and amongst my brother John Keayne's children that shall be then alive, and to be divided between them according to the discretion of my executor to give greater portions in the division thereof to them that stands in most need of it. And if my son do know any other of my poor kindred in Old England ... he [is to] give amongst them some part of this one hundred pounds besides the ten shillings apiece before mentioned, as he in his discretion and wisdom shall see cause.

Item. I give of it one hundred pounds amongst my overseers of this will equally to be divided between them.

And for the residue and remainder of all these general and public gifts before mentioned in this my will if any such thing should be attempted or endeavored to the disturbing or interrupting of the free passage of this my will or to the change and alteration thereof contrary to my true intent and meaning which doth cause or procure this alienation and change of that part of my will in such free gifts as I have before given to any particular town or place, to any particular society or company, or to any particular use or employment of those general gifts, save only that one hundred and twenty pounds that I have given to the school and poor in Boston and to particular friends—I say the residue and remaining part of these gifts and legacies not above disposed of I give and bequeath wholly to my son Benjamin Keayne and his peculiar use only.

[Last Minute Provisions]

Item. I give and bequeath unto Mr. Bellingham, our honored deputy, as a token of my love and respects to him forty shillings for a legacy to be paid to him two years after my decease if he be then alive and remaining in this country.

Item. I give and bequeath unto my dear friend Mr. Edward Winslow, now in Old England, as a token of my love and respects to him three pounds for a legacy to be paid him two years after my decease if he be then alive; if dead, then I give the same to his loving wife or eldest son. I do acknowledge myself greatly engaged to him for his care, counsel, and great love and respect that he hath showed to my son in England, though I had forgotten him before.

As for any legacy or legacies mentioned in this will and given to my cousin Benjamin Jupe and to my cousin Mary Morse, for some just occasions of offense that since have been given to me, I do hereby will and declare all such gifts before mentioned concerning them or either of them in this my will to become utterly void and of no effect in respect of them as if they had been never mentioned or given unto them, and not to be performed nor paid to them or either of them by my executor [unless] by some new act or declaration either by word of mouth before witness or some act or declaration under my own handwriting I shall give further order therein. This withdrawing of my gifts from them is not without some grief to myself for their sakes, but seeing they have pulled it upon themselves against my desire and have withdrawn themselves from that long care and tender love that I have borne to them in seeking and desiring their good for some private ends of their own, I think there is a period put to my further care over them by themselves. And if they receive any detriment by it they must blame themselves and not me.

And now things being thus willed, ordered, and concluded of by this my will I shall now draw to an end. It may be there are some other of my friends and acquaintance that I respect and might have expressed my love unto had they come into my memory, though my estate cannot reach to all according to the largeness of my desire and heart. For if it would I should leave out none that I have received any real love or courtesy from and it may be to my grief. I may think of some others that I have forgotten, but being forgot I hope they will not be offended with me or charge me with any ingratitude or want of love to them.

[Overseers Named]

And of this my last will and testament I make and appoint my only son Major Benjamin Keayne, as I have before said, to be my sole executor. It is contained in nine sheets of paper numbered to 36 pages or sides of paper, all of it, yea every line and word in it, being written with my own hand and my name subscribed at the lower end of every page, which shall be a sufficient sign and manifestation of it, to declare this to be my last will and testament and to stand and be performed as my last will. And I do by these presents revoke, null, and make void all former and other wills, gifts, and grants whatsoever heretofore by me made or any other will, if any other should be presented or pretended, that is not of my own handwriting, yea, [or] if anything should be drawn from me or expressed by me in my sickness or at my death when I may not have my memory and understanding fresh and free to contradict and overthrow this will which I have made and drawn up in my health and with my best understanding and memory suiting my own mind and desire. Therefore, I do make these presents to be and to contain my last will and testament in manner and form aforesaid.

And that all things in this my will may honestly and faithfully be performed so far as is possible according to my true desire and meaning, I do hereby ordain and appoint, constitute, yea, and also earnestly desire and request my honored and loving friends Mr. Simon Bradstreet, Major General Denison, his brother Mr. William Hibbins (three of our honored magistrates), also Mr. Edward Winslow of Plymouth, if he return back to abide in New England, also my dear brother Mr. John Wilson, pastor of Boston Church, and my loving friend Mr. Norton, minister, my loving cousin Mr. Edward Rawson, and Lieut. Johnson, our deacon, to be overseers of this my will. Unto all of these or any three or four of them I give power and authority to call my executor or others to an account if there should appear any neglect in him or them in the performance on his part and to see that this my will may carefully be accomplished. And [I] do earnestly desire them all and beseech them to be assistant to my executor and wife with their best aid, advice, counsel, and direction from time to time about the right disposing and best ordering of this my estate and to see my legacies disposed of according to my will as fast as things can be put off and payments come in, still with this [consideration], that neither my executor, wife, nor grandchild may be wronged in their parts or portions but provided for in the first place as is before expressed. And [I desire] that mine overseers would have an eye and look after Hannah Keayne, my grandchild, in respect of her education and training up in the fear of God as well as also in respect of marriage, if she live to such a condition, and to be helpful to her with their counsel and advice in such a choice, especially if God should take away her father or grandmother before, and not to suffer her to be drawn away by any such match as may apparently tend to the hurt or overthrow of her soul or body, but to hinder and make stop of any such motions to their utmost power.

And my desire is that my overseers would have three of four copies of this my will or of the most material parts of it (if they think the whole to be too long or needless) writ out at my charge to keep always by them to view and peruse upon any occasion when they meet together about it, or otherwise that they may the better take care to have the several particulars thereof performed. And ... because some legacies herein mentioned will or may prove somewhat large before they come to be accomplished, and because there is some legacies that depend upon accidental occasions, therefore if a few of them could be printed at no great charge I would think that the better way and then everyone that is concerned in the will may have a copy of the whole by him.

And what[ever] the greatest number of my overseers shall do when they meet together about any advice or counsel for the best disposing or managing of what I have left behind me to accomplish the true ends and intentions of this my will, taking therein also the advice and consent of my executor in their meetings and consultations, that shall stand and be accounted good. Yet I see not that it will be of absolute necessity that every one of my overseers should meet at all times or nothing can be carried on, though it would be very necessary that they would meet all together as often as there shall be any needful occasion. And if any of these overseers should die or remove out of the country, especially if the rest see a want of them, then my will and desire is that the surviving overseers with the advice and consent of my executor and my wife, would make choice of some other fit one in their rooms. And as a token of my love and thankfulness to them all for their foreseen care, pains, counsel, and faithfulness I do give and bequeath to each of them five pounds apiece in good pay to buy for everyone of them a piece of plate as a remembrance of my due respects unto them for that labor of love that I desire and expect from them in this business betrusted with them after my decease.

In witness that all things contained in this my last will and testament is my own act and deed and according to my mind, as I have set my name to every page in these nine sheets so in the last page of the last sheet I have put to my hand and seal the fourteenth day of November, one thousand six hundred fifty and three when I finished the same.

ROBERT KEAYNE   (seal)

Sealed, delivered, published, and declared this to be my last will and testament in the presence of us who testify that this writing or will contains nine sheets of paper written full on all sides.

JOHN WILSON   RICHD PARKER   EDW. TINGE

[*A Little Addition More*]

Perceiving that in the last sheet of my will, page 36, I am so much straitened that there is not convenient room left for the witnesses' hands, I have thought meet to begin another page in this sheet and to make a little addition more to the rest of my will in the former sheets of paper, having forgot one or two more that since came to my memory.

Item. I give and bequeath to James Bitts, the Scotchman, if he be in my service when I die, twenty shillings.

Item. I give and bequeath to Nan Ostler, my maidservant, twenty shillings, if she be in my service when I die.

I shall only add this, that it is very likely that those which come to hear or read over this my will may meet with some tautologies and some things that may be mentioned twice or thrice over in several places which they may think to be vain and needless repetitions, and some may possibly censure it to be a fruit of an unsettled mind or weak or wavering judgment as if I were not compos mentis when I made my will. But I would pray them not so to think but to impute it to the weakness and shortness of my memory, my will not being made at one time or in one day, for the length of it would not permit that, but at several times as I had leisure and opportunity to carry it on. [It was] begun mo. 6. 1. 1653 but not quite finished till November 15th, 1653, and this addition not till December 15, 1653, and so I might well forget some things that I had mentioned before, not having time at every time that I began to write to read over what I had before written. Yet sometimes I did remember and possibly perused what I had writ before of such a subject, but that not expressing my mind fully I bring in the same again that I might add somewhat more to it for the more full or clear expressing my mind or meaning therein.

Therefore, my request to all that shall hear or read this my will is that they will make a favorable construction of all things contained in it and to pass by all my human frailties and weaknesses therein and to take nothing in the worst sense where a more Christian and loving interpretation may be made of it, nor none to take or pick out of it anything of it to the prejudice of my will or the disappointing or frustrating of any of their right which I have given to them. ... If some words or expressions should seem to jar or differ [let] these ... be interpreted as near as can be gathered or reconciled with the scope of my will in general or other places of it in particular to be my true intent and meaning. For the will being long and my mind full of thoughts and exercises especially in some parts or passages in it there may be many defects in it that may justly call for a mantle of love to cover them, and it is like that had I time to copy it out fair again (which the length thereof will not easily permit, for I had many thoughts that I should have died before I had quite finished, having had one fit of sickness or weakness [that] lay sore upon me and long, which made me hasten the finishing of it all I could), I should leave out several things that are now in it. But I am not willing to employ anybody else to write it out but myself. Therefore, it must now pass with what faults or defects may be judged to be in it.

Item. I give to Mr. Bulkley, senior, minister of Concord, three pounds, and to Mr. Thompson, minister of Braintree, forty shillings, as tokens of my love.

I have forgot one loving couple more that came not to my mind till I was now shutting up and that is Capt. Bridges and his loving wife, to whom I give and bequeath forty shillings as a pledge of my loving respects to them, to be paid two years after my decease if then living and abiding in this country.

If my loving wife or any other should be offended that I have not made my wife executrix as I did when my son was under age or that I have not now joined her with my son in the executorship as I have done in some former wills, my son being then in the wars in England and so his life the more uncertain, [I say that] I conceive it not so convenient now, he being of full age and upon his return home. Therefore, [I have arranged things this way] to prevent differences that possibly might happen between my wife and her son, but chiefly because the accomplishment of this will will procure much care and some trouble and labor more fit for a man to undergo than a woman, and I think it would be too great a burden and work for her to undertake. Besides, if she should marry again before the will should be fully accomplished and fulfilled there might come some trouble to her and more inconvenience to my estate, of all which she is eased and may enjoy her own part and due in peace and quiet.

Therefore, I do here again declare all that which is contained before in nine sheets of paper writ with my own hand in all the sides thereof and more particularly expressed in the 36 pages thereof with all that is added to it in this page 37 to be my last will and testament and my son Major Benjamin Keayne to be sole executor thereof and my loving friends mentioned in the lower end of page 36 to be the overseers of it.

In witness whereof as there so here again I have put to my hand and seal in the presence of these whose names and hands are hereunder written this December 28, 1653.

ROBERT KEAYNE (seal)

JOHN WILLSON   EDW TING

RICHARD PARKER   ROBT HULL

                         EDW FFLETCHER